Building Skills for Black Workers

Preparing for the Future Labor Market

Edited by
Cecilia A. Conrad

**Joint Center for Political and Economic Studies™
Washington, DC**

University Press of America,® Inc.
Dallas · Lanham · Boulder · New York · Oxford

The Joint Center for Political and Economic Studies informs and illuminates the nation's major public policy debates through research, analysis, and information dissemination in order to: improve the socioeconomic status of black Americans and other minorities; expand their effective participation in the political and public policy arenas; and promote communications and relationships across racial and ethnic lines to strengthen the nation's pluralistic society.

Opinions expressed in Joint Center publications are those of the authors and do not necessarily reflect the views of the staff, officers, or governors of the Joint Center or of the organizations supporting the Joint Center and its research.

Copyright 2004 by the Joint Center for Political and Economic Studies™
1090 Vermont Avenue, NW, Suite 1100, Washington, DC 20005
www.jointcenter.org

Co-published by arrangement with the Joint Center for Political and Economic Studies, Inc.

University Press of America,® Inc.
4501 Forbes Boulevard, Suite 200
Lanham, Maryland 20706
UPA Acquisitions Department (301) 459-3366

PO Box 317
Oxford, OX2 9RU, UK

All rights reserved.
Printed in the United States of America.

British Library Cataloging in Publication Information Available
Library of Congress Control Number: 2003114220
ISBN 0-7618-2778-1 (clothbound: alk. ppr.)
ISBN 0-7618-2779-X (paperback: alk. ppr.)

The paper used in this publication meets the minimum requirements of American National Standard for Information Sciences*Permanence of Paper for Printed Library Materials, ANSI Z39.48*1984.

Contents

List of Figures and Tables   iv

Foreword   ix
Eddie N. Williams

Chapter 1. Introduction and Overview   1
Cecilia A. Conrad
   Figures and Tables   9
   Notes   14

**Chapter 2. The Effect of Class Size and
School Vouchers on Minority Achievement**   15
Cecilia Elena Rouse
   Figures and Tables   33
   Notes   45

**Chapter 3. The Digital Divide in Educating
Black Students and Workers**   51
Alan B. Krueger
   Tables   65
   Notes   75

**Chapter 4. Racial and Ethnic Differences in the
Impact of Job Training on Wages**   77
William M. Rodgers III
   Tables   89
   Notes   102

Chapter 5. Do Black Workers Lack Soft Skills?   105
Cecilia A. Conrad
   Notes   122

**Chapter 6. The Role of Public Policy in the Skills
Development of Black Workers in the 21st Century**   127
Timothy Bartik and Kevin Hollenbeck
   Notes   147

Bibliography   149

About the Authors   163

LIST OF FIGURES AND TABLES

Figure 1.1   [flow chart]. 9

Figure 1.2   Percent of High School Dropouts 10

Figure 1.3   Percent of 25-29-Year-Olds Who Have
Completed High School, by Race/Ethnicity 11

Figure 1.4   Percent of Persons Age 25 and Older Who
Have Completed 4 years of College,
by Race/Ethnicity. 12

Table 1.1   Work Related Training Experiences,
Spring 1993 13

Table 1.2   Racial Composition of Participants in
Government Training Programs 13

Figure 2.1   Average NAEP Reading Proficiency, by Age
and by Race/Ethnicity, 1970-1999 33

Figure 2.2   Average NAEP Mathematics Proficiency, by
Age and by Race/Ethnicity, 1971-1999. 34

Figure 2.3   The Percentage of Students Who Took the ACT
or SAT College Exam, by Initial Class Type 35

Figure 2.4   Understanding Individual Fixed-Effects 36

Figure 2.5   The Difference in Math Test Scores Between
Choice, City-Wide, P-5 Schools and "Regular"
Milwaukee Public Schools: African American
Students 37

Figure 2.6   The Difference in Math Test Scores Between
Choice, City-Wide, p-5 Schools and "Regular"
Milwaukee Public Schools: Hispanic Students . . 38

Table 2.1   The Effect of Small Class Sizes on Student
Achievement: Evidence From the Tennessee

	STAR Experiment	39
Table 2.2	The Effect of Randomized School Vouchers on School Quality: Evidence from the New York City School Choice Scholarships Program	40
Table 2.3	The Effect of Randomized School vouchers on Student Achievement: Evidence From the Dayton OH, New York City and Washington DC School Choice Scholarship Programs	41
Table 2.4	Mean Characteristics of Applicants to the Choice Program and Students in the Milwaukee Public Schools	42
Table 2.5	The Effect of Randomized School Vouchers on Student Achievement After Three Years: Evidence from the New York City School Choice Scholarship Program	43
Table 2.6	Individual Fixed-Effect (FE) Estimates of the Effect of Choice Schools, City-Wide, and P-5 Schools on Math and Reading Test Scores for African American and Hispanic students	44
Table 3.1	Percent of Students Using a Computer in School, by Race and Hispanic Origin	65
Table 3.2	Percent of Students Using the Internet in School, October 1997	66
Table 3.3	Linear Probability Model for Computer Use, 1984	67
Table 3.4	Linear Probability Model for Computer Use, 1989	68
Table 3.5	Linear Probability Model for Computer Use, 1993	69
Table 3.6	Linear Probability Model for Computer Use, 1997	70
Table 3.7	Percent of Workers Who Use a Computer	

                    at Work, 1997 71

Table 3.8   Uses of Computers at Work in1997,
                    by Race and Hispanic Origin 72

Appendix Table 3a   Standard Errors for Table 3.1 73

Appendix Table 3b   Sample Sizes for Table 3.1. 74

Table 4.1   The Incidence of Firm-Provided Job Training. . . 89

Table 4.2   Factors that Affect the Probability of
                    Training Receipt. 90

Table 4.3   Economic Returns to Schooling, Experience,
                    Tenure, Cognitive Skills 91

Table 4.4   Percentage Change in Worker Earnings
                    Associated With Firm Provided Training. 92

Table 4.5   Decomposition of Black-White Wage
                    Differences: Difference in Intercepts. 93

Table 4.6   Decomposition of Black-White Wage Gap
                    Discrimination as Differences in
                    Returns-to-Skill 94

Appendix Table 4A   Probit Estimates of the Determinants
                    of Training by Type 95

Appendix Table 4B   Returns to Schooling, Experience,
                    Tenure, Cognitive Skills and Firm
                    Provided Training. 97

Appendix Table 4C   Residence at Age 14 by Whether
                    Respondent Started School
                    Before 1964 98

Appendix Table 4D   Respondents that Started School
                    Prior to 1964 99

Appendix Table 4E: OLS, Random Effects, and Correlated . . . .
                      Random Effects Estimates of the Black-
                      White Wage Gap: Discrimination as . . . . .
                      Difference in Returns-to-Skill. 100

Appendix Table 4F   OLS, Random Effects, and Correlated
                      Random Effects Estimates of the Black-
                      White Wage Gap: Discrimination
                      as Difference in Intercepts 101

Table 5.1   Soft Skills Taxonomy 107

When we entered the 21st century, the U.S. unemployment rate was at a 30-year low of four percent. At the beginning of 2003, however, the rate was up to six percent. But good times or bad, the racial gap in unemployment has remained constant. African Americans are more than twice as likely to be unemployed as their white counterparts. While racial discrimination continues to play a role in causing this gap, it is clear that differences in education and training play a substantial role as well.

This volume, *Building Skills for Black Workers: Preparing for the Future Labor Market*, is the second in the Joint Center's series, The Black Worker in the 21st Century. The preceding volume, *Job Creation: Prospects and Strategies*, focused on the demand side—increasing the numbers of job opportunities for African Americans. However, job creation alone will not solve the employment problems of black workers. Higher levels of education and technical skill are required for the new century's better-paying jobs, and African Americans still lag behind in acquiring what is needed.

The authors in this book focus on different aspects of education and training—including in-school education, government training programs, and employer-provided opportunities. Given the likelihood that workers will face several career changes over their work lives, a substantial portion of the labor force will need access to all three types of training. This volume explores the extent to which the opportunities are currently available to African Americans and strategies that will improve their access to the training necessary to advance their careers.

The idea for a series of publications on policies affecting black workers in this century originated with a grant from the Rockefeller Foundation. This specific volume took shape with a conference sponsored by the U.S. Department of Labor, at which early versions of the chapters were presented and discussed. The Joint Center would like to thank both the Rockefeller Foundation and the Labor Department for their early support, and also thank our general support donors for enabling us to see the work through to completion.

In addition to the volume editor, Cecilia A. Conrad, and the chapter authors, we would like to thank those individuals who provided formal comments on early drafts. They include Eileen Appelbaum, Sheila Ards, David Brown, Anthony Carnevale, Robert Lerman, Susan McElroy, Glenda Partee, Steven Savner, and Sue Stockly. Finally, I would like to thank Margaret Simms, senior vice president for programs, for her continued leadership of our economic policy work, and Denise Dugas, vice president for communications and marketing, and her staff for producing another high-quality publication.

Eddie N. Williams
President
Joint Center for Political and Economic Studies

Chapter One

INTRODUCTION AND OVERVIEW

Cecilia A. Conrad

For African Americans, the economic prosperity of the 1990s led to an expansion of employment opportunities. The black unemployment rate averaged around 7.6 percent from January 2000 to November 2000 — the lowest rate in over twenty years. However, this good economic news should not be cause for complacency. Racial differences in employment and wages continue to be significant. African Americans remain more than twice as likely to be unemployed as white workers and they are more likely to work in lower-paid, lower-skilled jobs. In 1998, an African American male earned an average 72 cents for every dollar earned by a white, non-Hispanic male — roughly the same gap as in 1968.

One explanation for this persistent disparity in economic status is a persistent gap in education and training. Despite recent improvements in educational attainment, black workers still lag behind whites in college completion rates and in other indicators of academic achievement. Survey evidence suggests that employers have negative perceptions of the basic skills of African American workers, including soft skills such as verbal communication and teamwork. Any elixir for improving the economic status of African American workers and their families must address the problems of black workers who lack the skills needed to compete in the competitive market of the 21st century.

This volume assesses the current gap in education and training between African American and white workers and explores possible remedies. It begins with an examination of the elementary and secondary education system (K-12) and concludes with an analysis of public and private worker training programs. The chapters address three broad questions.

- How do workers acquire the skills needed for upward mobility and career advancement?

Cecilia A. Conrad is the Stedman-Sumner professor of economics at Pomona College and the editor of this volume.

- What is the current gap in education and training between black and white workers?
- What strategies would reduce the gaps and improve the labor market outcomes for these workers?

Cecilia Rouse (Chapter 2) describes racial differences in K-12 student achievement and summarizes the effectiveness of class size reduction and voucher initiatives. Alan Krueger (Chapter 3) documents the digital divide in K-12 classrooms and discusses its implications for employment and earnings. William Rodgers' (Chapter 4) focus is the racial difference in participation in employer provided training programs. Cecilia Conrad (Chapter 5) examines racial differences in intangible, soft skills. Finally, Timothy Bartik and Kevin Hollenbeck (Chapter 6) provide an overview of federal, state, and local government involvement in skill development. This introductory chapter provides a broad overview of racial differences in educational attainment and participation in both private and public skill improvement training.

THE SKILL DEVELOPMENT SYSTEM IN THE UNITED STATES

Bartik and Hollenbeck characterize the current system for skill development in the United States as a two tiered system. The "first chance" or conventional system allows individuals to proceed through an extensive public elementary, secondary, and postsecondary educational sector that is supplemented by private educational institutions and is followed by employer-provided job training and work experience. A second chance system provides job training for those workers not well served by the first chance system. This second chance system comprises public job training programs, public assistance, rehabilitation programs and educational remediation programs.

Figure 1.1 describes this two-tiered skill development system. The point of entry for both tiers is the K-12 educational system.[1] Students who exit this system without a traditional high school diploma face three possible paths. One path leads directly into the formal labor market, into dead-end jobs that offer no chance for upward mobility. A second path leads into informal work and non-work activity. A third leads into the second chance system. The second chance system offers an opportunity for many to complete a General Education Degree (GED). Of the 1990 cohort of high school sophomores who dropped out of high school, over half had completed their high school education two years later, 11 percent with an alternative credential.[2] (Although employers tend to value a GED less than a traditional high school diploma, the degree provides an opportunity for some to flow back into the first chance system — primarily into two-year college and vocational programs.

Students who graduate with a traditional high school diploma have four pathways. The first is directly into the formal labor market. In the diagram, they enter the labor market at a slightly higher rung than do those who completed high school through the second chance system. A second path is into two-year community colleges and vocational schools. A third path is directly into a four-year college or university.[3]

Some traditional high school graduates will still end up in the second chance system because of the poor quality of schooling they received. In national inventories of the workplace skills for the 21st century, employers express concerns about the basic skills and soft skills of US workers. Basic skills (reading, writing, and arithmetic) and soft skills (verbal communication skills, problem solving and practical cognition, interpersonal and teamwork skills and personal qualities and work ethic) are generally acquired through the K-12 system. These basic skills are required for workers to be able to learn new tasks and to acquire more specialized knowledge. Workers who do not acquire these basic skills through their K-12 education may not be able to find employment or may find their labor market opportunities as limited as those of school leavers.

Skill development does not end with formal schooling. Once in the workforce, workers acquire additional skills through informal and formal job training. Economists divide this work-related training into two broad categories — firm-specific skill training and general training. Firm-specific skill training enhances a worker's value to a specific employer. General skills training increases the worker's value to any employer. In theory, employers will tend to invest in firm specific skill development and workers (or taxpayers) must pay for the development of general skills. Estimates of the provision of formal training by employers vary, but in a 1995 survey by the U.S. Bureau of Labor Statistics, 93 percent of employers with 50 or more employees reported provision of formal job training in the past twelve months. Almost 70 percent of employees received formal training during that time.[4]

RACIAL GAPS IN EDUCATION AND TRAINING: THE FIRST CHANCE SYSTEM

Thanks to over two decades of declining dropout rates, African Americans now have high school completion rates comparable to those of whites. Figure 1.2 reports the status dropout rate. Status dropouts are 16-24 year olds who are not enrolled in school and who have not completed a high school program regardless of when they left school. From the 1960's through 1998, the status dropout rate of African Americans declined dramatically, narrowing the gap with whites. Even though dropout rates have recently increased, the increase has been smaller for African Americans. Hence, the racial gap has not widened. Another indicator of educational attainment paints a similar picture. Figure 1.3 reports the high school completion rates of 25-29 year olds.

The convergence in high school completion rates is good news, but its potential impact on racial earnings inequality is neutralized by a second phenomenon — the rising wage premium for college educated labor.[5] College completion rates of African Americans continue to lag behind those of whites. Figure 1.4 describes this trend by race and ethnicity. During the 1980s, college completion rates of whites increased while those of African Americans and Hispanics were relatively stagnant. The college completion rate of African Americans is less than 60 percent that of whites.

The reasons for this gap in college completion rates are complex. Some observers finger failures in the K-12 education system. Blacks are less likely to complete a college preparatory curriculum in high school.[6] Blacks have lower average scores on college entrance exams. Because they typically enter college with weaker credentials, retention rates in four-year colleges are lower for African Americans. Of the African American high school graduates who do pursue postsecondary education, the majority attend two-year community colleges and other vocational education programs.

Not all the news on K-12 schooling is bad. Rouse's chapter details improvements in math and reading test scores of African American students. Between 1971 and 1999, the reading test scores of African American students increased by 7 percent for 13 year olds and by 10 percent for 17 year olds. The reading scores of white students increased by 1-3 percent. Nevertheless, the gaps that remain are significant.

In addition to the gaps in reading and mathematics achievement, there is a digital divide in K-12 schooling, but, according to Krueger, this is also narrowing. In 1984, black students were 16 percentage points less likely than white students were to use a computer in school and only 6 percentage points less likely in 1997. The black-white gap in the proportion of students who use a computer in school completely disappeared by 1997 for high school students while a 10-point gap remains for students in grades 1-8. Hispanic students were 13.5 percentage points less likely than whites to use a computer in school in 1984 and 7 percentage points less likely in 1997.

AFRICAN AMERICANS IN THE SECOND CHANCE SYSTEM

As a result of the failures in the K-12 educational system, many African Americans end up in what Bartik and Hollenbeck label the "second chance" system. Table 1.1 describes racial differences in participation in work-related training programs. In 1993, the proportion of whites and blacks with work-related training were identical — 27 percent. However, a higher proportion of blacks received their training through federal, state and local government programs. Forty-five percent of blacks reported participation in public work-related training programs compared with 22 percent of whites. In contrast, 51 percent of whites reported participation in employer provided training compared with only 33 percent of blacks. A smaller proportion of Hispanics than either blacks or whites reported any work-related training — 19 percent. The proportions of Hispanics with employer provided training and public training were similar — 36 percent and 38 percent respectively.

Rodgers' analysis data from the National Longitudinal Survey of Youth also finds differences in participation by race. White men and women have the highest company training participation rates. The participation rates of white men and women are 2.2 percentage points higher than the rate of African American men and just over 0.7 percentage points higher than the rate of African American women. The other largest racial gap in training is in seminars outside of work. Between 3 and 4 percent of white men and women reported participating in seminars outside of work, compared to 1.0 to 1.7 for African American men and women. African Americans have slightly higher participation rates in vocational programs.

Black workers are over-represented in government programs for disadvantaged workers. Table 1.2 reports the participation in JTPA and Job Corps programs by race. African Americans made up nearly 45 percent of JTPA Title II program terminees and 27 percent of eligible Job Corp applicants.

Most workers, regardless of race, acquire their skills through the first chance system, but African Americans are disproportionately represented in the second chance system. Thus, African Americans have a vital interest in the operation of this second chance system.

STRATEGIES FOR SKILL DEVELOPMENT OF AFRICAN AMERICAN WORKERS

Although by some indicators racial gaps in education and training are narrowing, the differences that remain contribute to black-white inequality today and will continue to do so in the future. Krueger argues that workers who possess computer skills tend to fare better in the labor market than seemingly identical workers without those skills. Conrad cites evidence that employers are willing to pay a higher wage for workers who possess soft skills. Thus, improving the economic status of African American workers depends critically on improving the skills they bring to the labor market.

The papers included in this volume offer some important lessons about how to address the remaining skill deficits through the public sector and the private sector. Some findings challenge conventional thinking. For example, in contrast with earlier studies of the link between school resources and student achievement, Rouse finds that class-size matters. It especially matters for African Americans. Based on results from the Tennessee Student/Teacher Achievement (STAR) experiment, she concludes that class size reductions can increase student performance on standardized tests and increase the probability that a student will take a college entrance exam. The STAR results suggest that being assigned to a small class narrows the gap between African Americans and whites in college test taking by just over one-half.

Rodgers' chapter challenges mainstream thinking on black-white earnings inequality. Recent studies argue that pre-market factors — family inputs and school quality — explain nearly one-hundred percent of black-white earnings differences. Rodgers' results refute this argument. After controlling for pre-market factors, participation in formal training programs and work experience, he reports a black-white wage gap of 6.5 percent for women and 10.5 percent for men. While this suggests that on-the-job or business-provided training cannot overcome discrimination or differential opportunity in other areas, Rodgers' analysis does show that blacks are less likely to receive the type of training that has the bigger payoffs.

A trend in both the first and second chance skill development systems is greater reliance on the private market for the provision of education and training and greater reliance on the individual to make choices. In Milwaukee and other communities, scholarship programs enable some low-income students to attend private schools. The Workforce Investment Act proposes a system of vouchers to finance education and training for disadvantaged workers. Three evaluations of the achievement effects of the Milwaukee Parental Choice Program report conflicting results. Rouse speculates that some of the gains in achievement test scores reported in choice schools may be the result of reductions in class size rather than privatization.

Bartik and Hollenbeck, as well as Conrad, stress the importance of addressing the problem of imperfect information along with the skill deficits of workers. Imperfect information is a factor in both sides of the labor market. Workers may lack information about the skills that employers demand. Employers lack information about the skills that workers bring to the labor market, especially their soft skills. This imperfect information is particularly likely to restrict job opportunities for African Americans as employers use race as a proxy for unobservable worker attributes.

School-to-work programs that link classroom based education with experiential learning through internships, mentor programs and jobs can address information imperfections on both sides of the markets. The programs give employers an opportunity to observe potential workers before they commit to employment, and they provide individuals with information about what employers want. In addition, school-to-work programs have another attribute identified by Bartik and Hollenbeck as essential for effective training programs. They provide on-going mentoring and counseling. Preliminary studies, cited both by Conrad and by Bartik and Hollenbeck, suggest that these programs are improving career development experiences for participants and are engaging a diverse population of students.

Krueger's research suggests a three-pronged strategy to improve computer literacy among African American students. A first step is to increase resources to purchase computers in schools predominately attended by minority students. A less obvious second step is to provide more training in computer use among teachers in schools that are attended by minority students. Krueger's chapter also highlights the need for additional research on the link between computer assisted instruction and student performance and the link between computer use in K-12 schools and an individual's employability.

CONCLUSIONS

The racial gap in skills has narrowed, but in the competitive market of the 21st century, the skill differences that remain are more important than ever before. This growing importance of skill, coupled with the persistence of labor market discrimination, has contributed to a persistence of black-white earnings differences. In the competitive workplace of the new millennium, the probability of economic success for minority workers is likely to be even more dependent on the skills they bring to the marketplace and on their ability to acquire new skills to adapt to the rapidly changing economic environment. With minorities a larger proportion of the overall workforce, the creation of opportunities and incentives for minority workers to improve their skills is an important part of improving the overall productivity of the economy.

FIGURE 1.1

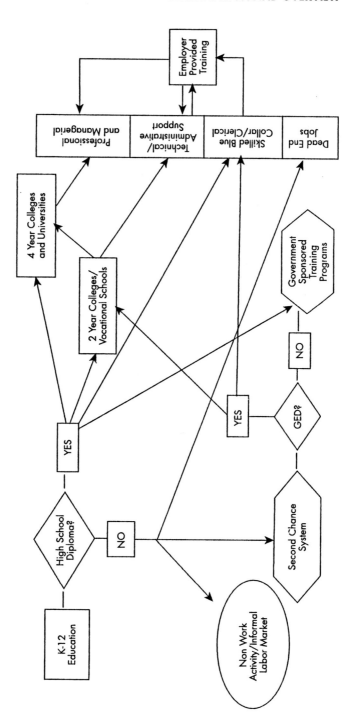

FIGURE 1.2
PERCENT OF HIGH SCHOOL DROPOUTS
(STATUS DROPOUTS)

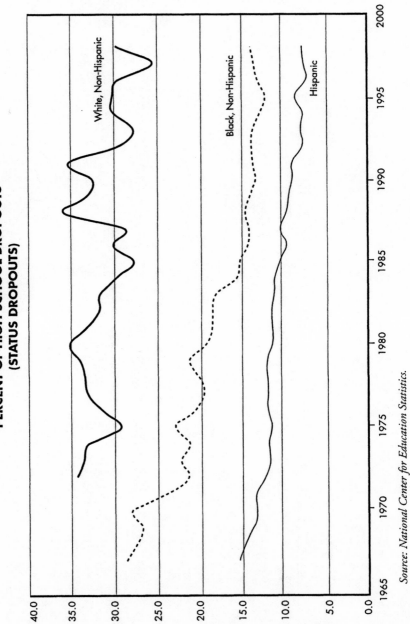

Source: National Center for Education Statistics.

FIGURE 1.3
PERCENT OF 25-29-YEAR-OLDS WHO HAVE
COMPLETED HIGH SCHOOL, BY RACE/ETHNICITY

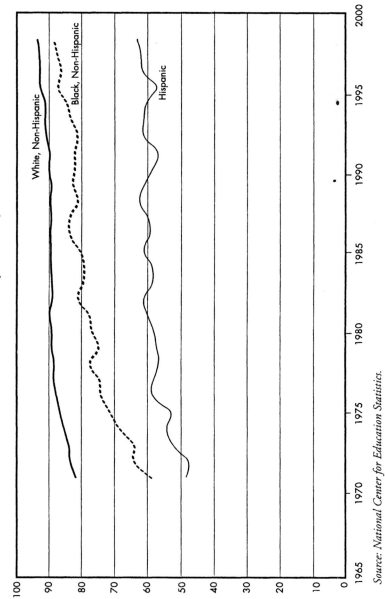

Source: National Center for Education Statistics.

FIGURE 1.4
PERCENT OF PERSONS AGE 25 AND OLDER WHO HAVE
COMPLETED 4 YEARS OF COLLEGE, BY RACE/ETHNICITY

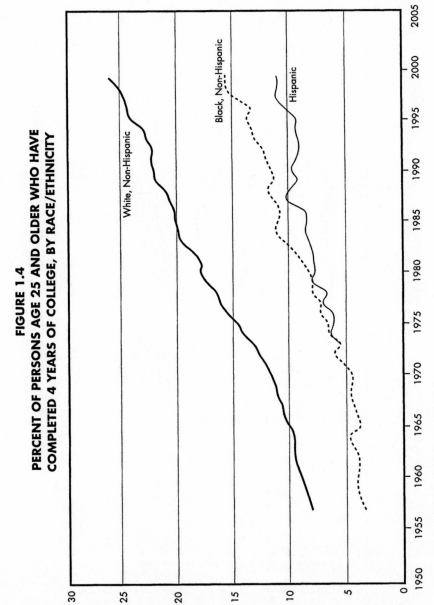

Source: National Center for Education Statistics.

TABLE 1.1

WORK RELATED TRAINING EXPERIENCES, SPRING 1993

	Total Population	White	Black	Hispanic Origin
Total with Work related training	42,225	35,736	5,063	2,830
Total with work related training as proportion of population aged 18-64	0.27%	0.27%	0.27%	0.19%
Proportion of population with work related training, employer provided	0.48	0.51	0.33	0.36
Proportion of population with work related training: federal, state or local govt	0.25	0.22	0.45	0.38

Source: _http://www.census.gov/population/socdemo/education/table07.txt_ retrieved March 28, 1999

TABLE 1.2

RACIAL COMPOSITION OF PARTICIPANTS IN GOVERNMENT TRAINING PROGRAMS

	All JTPA Programs	JTPA, Title II-A	JTPA- Title II-C	Job Corps (Eligible Applicants)
Black	54.6%	44.6%	38.0%	27.0
Hispanic Origin	25.5	34.1	33.3	47.7
White	15.3	16.8	23.7	17.7
Other	4.6	4.4	5.0	7.6

Sources: _JTPA terminee data from Social Policy Research Associates, "PY 97 SPIR Data Book" (1999) ; Job Corps data from Peter Schochet, "National Job Corps Study" (1998)._

NOTES

1. Programs like Head Start that focus on pre-K skill development are important, but beyond the scope of this volume.

2. U.S. Department of Education, National Center for Education Statistics," Later Completions by Dropouts, " http://www.nces.ed.gov/pubs2000/coe2000/charts/charts20.html, retrieved December 27, 2000.

3. For simplicity, the diagram does not depict career paths for those who drop out of the postsecondary education system. It also does not depict the path into post baccalaureate studies.

4. Harley Frazis, Maury Gittleman, Michael Horrigan, and Mary Joyce, "Results from the 1995 Survey of Employer-Provided Training." *Monthly Labor Review,* June 1998 (vol. 121, no. 6).

5. In 1972, th e estimated premium for college-educated workers was 9 percent; by 1992, it was 36 percent.

6. National Center for Education Statistics, *Digest of Education Statistics,* 1999, table 142.

Chapter Two

THE EFFECT OF CLASS SIZE AND SCHOOL VOUCHERS ON MINORITY ACHIEVEMENT

Cecilia Elena Rouse

INTRODUCTION

Many argue that our schools are in crisis, particularly those attended by poor inner-city and rural children. The popular image is of crumbling schools that are ineptly and inefficiently run, resulting in children unable to learn and a cycle of poverty that is perpetuated. The gap in student outcomes by race and ethnicity is often cited as evidence of this crisis. For example, in 1997, 93 percent of whites aged 25-29 had attained a high school diploma or equivalency degree compared to 87 percent of African Americans and just 62 percent of Hispanics. Among those with a high school degree, 35 percent of whites had completed a bachelor's degree or higher compared to just 16 percent of African Americans and 18 percent of Hispanics.[1] Given the increasing importance of skills in our labor market, these gaps in educational attainment translate into large differences by race and ethnicity in eventual labor market outcomes, such as wages and employment.[2]

Many policymakers, believing that the status quo is unacceptable and that the stakes are increasing, have turned to different models of school reform in an attempt to improve our schools.[3] Examples of the reforms that are currently considered promising are whole-school reforms, charter schools,[4] class size reduction, and school vouchers. Although whole-school and charter school reforms are likely to become even more important in the 21st century, both are

---

Cecilia Elena Rouse is a professor of economics and public affairs at Princeton University and director of the Princeton University Education Research Section.

relatively new and have not yet been fully evaluated.[5] Therefore, the rest of this paper focuses on two methods of school reform: class size reduction and school vouchers. I begin by reviewing the current state of education as shown in the trends in (short-run) student achievement reported in the results of the National Assessment for Education Progress (NAEP). These trends suggest that the test scores of minority students have been converging with those of white students over the past 25 years, although large gaps still remain. As a result, it does not appear that our schools are actually performing worse than before, but there is still much work to be done to ensure that all children can obtain a quality education.

The remaining sections of the paper consider the evidence on class size reduction and "school choice" (vouchers). The best available evidence, which is from the Tennessee Student/Teacher Achievement Ratio (STAR) experiment, indicates that smaller class sizes do lead to improved student achievement, particularly for inner-city and minority children. In addition, results from randomized voucher experiments and the Milwaukee Parental Choice program suggest that providing vouchers to students to attend private schools may confer some advantage to those who use them, at least for African Americans. However, the reason that voucher schools may be better than non-voucher schools is unknown, although one possibility is their smaller class sizes. I conclude by highlighting the outstanding questions with regard to both of these reforms.

THE CURRENT STATE OF EDUCATION

The NAEP is a test in mathematics, reading, science, and writing administered to a nationally representative sample of 9-, 13-, and 17-year-olds approximately every two years. Because it is designed to be compared over time (unlike the Scholastic Achievement Test [SAT]), most analysts agree that the NAEP is a fairly good short-run barometer of the health of our nation's educational system.[6] Figures 2.1 and 2.2 show the trends in NAEP mathematics and reading scores from 1971 to 1999, by race and ethnicity. As shown in Figure 2.1, between 1971 and 1999 the reading test scores of African American students increased by between 7 percent (for 13-year-olds) and 10 percent (for 17-year-olds), although the improvement was not steady throughout the time period. The increases in math, shown in Figure 2.2, were similar. The test scores for Hispanics have also increased since the 1970s, although not as dramatically (with a range between 5 percent and 7.5 percent). In contrast, the test scores of white students have been relatively constant. For example, their reading scores increased only about 1-3 percent, and their math scores increased by 3-4 percent for teenagers and 7 percent for 9-year-olds. These figures suggest that the achievement gap in math and reading between whites and African Americans and Hispanics has narrowed over the past 25 years.[7] However, a substantial gap remains. Among 9-year-olds, white students scored about 12 to 13 percent higher than African American and Hispanic students in math in 1999 and from 14 to 19 percent higher in reading.

And absolute levels of achievement have been low. This is highlighted by the mediocre performance of the U.S. on international comparisons of test scores in math and science.[8] The contrast of these two trends, that the achievement gap by race/ethnicity has narrowed but a large gap remains, leads analysts to conflicting conclusions about the state of education in the U.S. Some researchers, such as Eric Hanushek, conclude that the sizable racial and ethnic gap in test scores and the overall low performance of all U.S. students suggest that our educational system is in serious need of change and that reforms that have been tried in the past (e.g., class size reduction, merit pay, increased spending) do not work.[9] Other researchers focus on the relative convergence in outcomes between African Americans (in particular) and whites. Alan Krueger notes that because the proportion of minority students who are immigrants or raised in poverty is rising, the trend in their test scores may understate the overall contribution of the schools. In addition, he argues that changes in NAEP scores are correlated with increases in school expenditures per student and decreases in pupil-teacher ratios.[10] As a result, perhaps our educational system is not in crisis, and traditional reforms can make a difference.

DO TRADITIONAL REFORMS WORK?

A direct assessment of whether traditional reforms, such as class size reduction or increased spending, are effective would correlate student outcomes to school inputs. The biggest challenge in such a study is to isolate the effect of the input, per se, from other factors such as family background. For example, families who have greater resources or who value schooling more highly may choose to live in school districts with better inputs (such as smaller class sizes); therefore, the effect of the inputs would be overstated because it would also include the effect of family background, which most agree is the most important determinant of student outcomes. In contrast, within schools, students needing compensatory education classes (such as special, bilingual, or remedial education) often receive greater inputs (such as smaller classes), and the effect of these inputs may be understated.

Consider a study of the effect of class size on student achievement. Ideally, to test whether smaller classes improve student achievement, one would have to know the achievement of the students when they are put in small classes and their achievement had they remained in larger classes. This counterfactual (the achievement of students in small classes if they had remained in larger classes) would provide a yardstick against which to measure the effect of class size. Because the counterfactual is impossible to observe, it is necessary to identify a group of students who remained in larger classes and whose test scores can provide the yardstick against which to measure the effect of class size; these students constitute a control or comparison group.

Many researchers would argue that using a randomized experiment is the best way to construct a control group. To determine whether the achievement of students improves when they are in smaller classes, one would randomly divide a group of students into two groups: One group is assigned to a small class (the treatment group); the others remain in the larger class (the control group). After some period of time, one would compare the outcomes (e.g., test scores, high school graduation rates, or labor market success) of both groups. Because, on average, the only difference between the groups would be their initial assignment, which was randomly determined, any differences in outcomes could be attributed to the difference in class size.

Probably the best evidence to date on the effect of small classes comes from just such an experimental design: the Tennessee Student/Teacher Achievement Ratio experiment, Project STAR. This is the largest randomized experiment aimed at understanding the effect of smaller class sizes on student achievement ever conducted in the United States.[11] In the 1985-1986 school year, approximately 6,000 kindergarten students in Tennessee were randomly assigned to one of three groups: small classes (13-17 students per teacher), regular-sized classes (22-25 students), and regular-sized classes (22-25 students) with a teacher's aide; over the length of the experiment, approximately 11,600 children were involved.[12] After being followed for four years, the students in the small classes returned to regular-sized classes for fourth grade. A variety of researchers have analyzed the data from Project STAR, and the results have been remarkably consistent.[13] The results from the most recent evaluation by Alan Krueger are shown in Table 2.1.[14] This table shows the effect of the small classes on the students' percentile rankings on the Stanford Achievement Test.

The results in column (1) show that students who were initially placed in a small class scored about 3 percentile points more than students in the regular-sized classes (including those that had a teacher's aid). In addition, each year in a small class yielded an increase of another 0.65 percentile points. Thus, after one year in a small class, students were scoring an additional 3.6 percentile points higher than those in larger classes. The results in the remaining columns in the table highlight one other result from this study: Small classes were particularly beneficial for low-income (i.e., those eligible for the free lunch program) and African American students and students attending inner-city schools. In fact, after one year, African American students placed in small classes scored 4.9 points higher than students placed in regular-sized classes; their test scores were about 1 point higher in each of the subsequent years. And these results are substantively large. For example, the achievement gains were about 0.18 of the standard deviation of the average percentile score. And the impact of being assigned to a small class in kindergarten was about 64 percent of the white-African American test score gap; in the third grade it was about 82 percent.

Despite the seemingly large impacts on test scores, it is unclear how test scores translate into factors (such as educational attainment and wages) that have more of a proven track record of mattering for success in later life. In a follow-up study of students participating in Project STAR, Krueger and Diane Whitmore studied the impact of being assigned to a small class on whether the students took either the SAT or ACT college entrance exam and how well they did. Krueger and Whitmore argue that sitting for a college entrance exam is correlated to some extent (although not perfectly) with eventual educational attainment and therefore provides an early indicator of long-run effects of the experiment. Figure 2.3 shows their results: On average, students assigned to small classes were almost 4 percentage points more likely to sit for a college entrance exam than those who were not assigned to a small class; among African Americans the increase was more than 8 percentage points. The magnitude of these differences suggests that being assigned to a small class narrows the African American-white gap in college test-taking by just over one-half. The authors also find evidence that students assigned to the small classes scored higher (by about 10 percent of a standard deviation on average, and twice that for African Americans) on the exams than those in regular-sized classes.[15]

Although the results from Project STAR suggest that there may be benefits to small classes, reducing class size is difficult and expensive to implement on a large scale because additional teachers must be hired and classrooms built. A good illustration of the potential difficulties in implementation is the experience of California. Since 1996, California has appropriated approximately $1.5 billion annually to reduce class size to 20 students or fewer in kindergarten through the third grade. While there are limited reports that teachers in smaller classes are actually changing their teaching practices, and parents are quite enthusiastic about the policy, schools and districts also report hiring less qualified teachers, holding classes in nontraditional spaces such as libraries and auditoriums, and doubling up classes so that two teachers and 40 students share a room.[16] The early results suggest some modest improvement in student test scores,[17] but it is too early to evaluate the long-run impact of the policy.

The average expenditure per student in the U.S. in 1997-98 was $6,624; reducing class sizes by about one-third (the average in the STAR experiment) would likely increase yearly costs by about $2,208.[18] Although Krueger performs a "back-of-the-envelope" calculation that suggests that the benefits of class size reduction may balance the costs,[19] the question remains whether this relatively expensive intervention is the most efficient use of public funds to improve education.

SCHOOL CHOICE

Reducing class size is expensive, and policymakers believe that it, along with other traditional reforms (e.g., merit pay), will not fix an educational system that is "broken." As a consequence, many states, such as Florida and Pennsylvania, have adopted or are considering programs that would provide vouchers for children (generally from low-income families) to attend private schools. Advocates of vouchers argue that teachers' unions and bloated bureaucracies impede traditional reforms, such as reducing class sizes, from reaching the classroom and increasing student achievement. Furthermore, because children are required to attend their neighborhood school, the system has no incentive to change.[20] While wealthier parents can voice dissatisfaction with their residential school by moving to another neighborhood or enrolling their child in a private school, poor parents, particularly those in the inner city, cannot afford to do so. Vouchers would, at a minimum, provide disadvantaged children with more educational options. If, in addition, they were to receive a better education in the private schools, the program may offer a cost-effective way to improve student achievement, at least for those students who use the vouchers.

Some argue that an unrestricted voucher program would also improve the schooling of all children. In the most unrestricted program, all (or a substantial fraction) of the students in the public schools would be eligible to attend a private school. Because state funding would be tied to student enrollments, the public schools would have to compete for students, as in the marketplace, and this would give the public schools an incentive to improve. If such an unrestricted voucher program were successful, one should observe improvement in the achievement not only of students who use the vouchers but also of students who are eligible but do not use them (i.e., the students who are "left behind" in the public school. In fact, in the long run, the academic outcomes of students in public and private schools should converge.

To date, the only attempts to study these systemic effects employ an indirect approach by looking for naturally occurring sources of school choice and competition.[21] In these studies, the authors do not look at the programs in which students are given vouchers to attend private (or better performing public) schools. Rather, they attempt to infer the likely effect of a voucher program by studying how public schools respond when they face more competitive pressure. Thus, these authors attempt to estimate the effect of competition on public school efficiency by testing whether student outcomes (or school quality) differ between areas with lots of competition (generated by many school districts or private schools) and areas with little competition. The inference is that if public schools appear to perform better when faced with more competition, then one would expect public schools to also improve under a voucher program. These studies generally conclude that more competition improves student achievement (or school quality) in public schools.

I do not focus on these studies in this paper primarily because, in order to infer that a voucher program would produce similar results, one must assume that the primary mechanism by which vouchers would improve education is through competitive pressure. However, it is unclear that public schools would respond as hypothesized because, for example, they are not "profit-maximizing" enterprises and the nature and extent of their responses to competitive pressures would likely depend critically on the parameters of the specific voucher program.[22]

Instead, I focus on evidence from direct studies of school vouchers — that is, studies of programs in which students were given vouchers to help subsidize the tuition at a private school. It is important to emphasize, however, that the existing school voucher programs are too small to provide insight into the potential student achievement benefits of an unrestricted voucher program. Evidence from these programs cannot show whether providing vouchers would also improve the schooling of students who remain in the public schools. However, analysis of the existing programs could indicate whether the private schools participating in the program (the voucher schools) are "better" than the public schools.

Randomized Experiments: School Choice Scholarships Programs in Dayton, Ohio; New York City; and Washington, DC

As in research on the effect of class size, in order to study whether vouchers would improve the achievement of students who use them to attend private schools, one would have to know the achievement of these students once in the private schools and their achievement had they remained in their assigned public schools. And many would argue that the best control group is constructed by using a randomized experiment in which one group of students is randomly selected to receive vouchers (the treatment group) and a second group of students is randomly selected not to receive vouchers (the control group).

This experiment was conducted in New York City by the School Choice Scholarships Foundation (SCSF) as well as in Dayton, Ohio, and Washington, D.C. The oldest and largest of these programs, in New York City, began in the spring of 1997 and provided scholarships worth up to $1,400 annually, for students initially in grades one to five, which could be used at both religious and secular private schools.[23] When the program accepted students (in the spring of 1997), only families that qualified for the federal free lunch program were eligible, as long as they had a child currently enrolled in a public school and lived in New York City. In order to participate in the final lottery, families had to participate in "eligibility verification" sessions at which the families completed surveys and their children were administered the Iowa Tests of Basic Skills. From over 20,000 initial applications, only 1,400 children were randomly assigned to receive a voucher or not. The experiments in the other two cities were similar.

A report on the results after three years was issued by Mathematica Policy Research; Table 2.2 shows some of their results.[24] Column (1) reports averages for students *offered* a voucher (whether they used it or not), and column (2) reports the difference between those offered a voucher and those not offered a voucher. The results in column (3) show averages for students who *actually* attended a voucher school (who actually used a voucher); column (4) reports the difference between those who used a voucher and those who did not.

The difference between the estimates in columns (1) and (2) and those in columns (3) and (4) derives from an issue common to randomized experiments: Randomization must occur at some point in the experiment. This fact affects the inferences one can make about both the program and the population to which the results apply. In the New York City experiment, the randomization occurred after parents had indicated substantial interest in the program. As a result, the estimates reflect the effect of being selected to receive a voucher among students already interested in attending a private school; they do not necessarily reflect the effect of having attended a private school because students who were offered a voucher may not have actually used it.[25] Similarly, some students in the control group may have attended a private school even though they did not receive a voucher (in fact, 12 percent of the control group enrolled in a private school for at least one year *without* a scholarship from the School Choice Scholarships Program). Nevertheless, because many policymakers are interested in whether *use* of a voucher improves student achievement, Mayer and his colleagues attempt to answer this question with the results in columns (3) and (4).[26] It is important to emphasize, however, that in this case the researchers must implicitly resort to a nonexperimental statistical methodology because students were not randomly assigned to actually *enroll* — or not enroll — in a voucher school or another private school. In addition, because all students in the experiment had expressed considerable interest in attending a private school, the effects are not necessarily those one would obtain for the general population.

It is evident from the first row of Table 2.2 that students who were offered a voucher attended smaller schools (with almost 100 fewer students or about 17 percent smaller) than those who were denied a voucher. Similarly, those offered a voucher attended schools with statistically smaller class sizes (with one fewer student, on average) than those denied vouchers. Other rows in the table indicate that the voucher schools were also significantly less likely to offer programs for non-English speakers and for the learning disabled although there were no (statistical) differences between the voucher and public schools in the likelihood of offering special programs for advanced learners. The fact that it appears that the public schools are more likely than the voucher schools to have special accommodations for compensatory education may be evidence that public schools educate a more heterogeneous population than private schools. This is one argument used by opponents of vouchers who argue that one cannot easily judge the effectiveness of public schools relative to private schools because the private schools can choose which students to educate.[27]

Another concern voiced by opponents is that school vouchers will increase racial and social segregation. Note, however, that there are few differences between those offered a voucher and those denied one in the percentage of students in the class of the same race/ethnic background as the child in question. Thus, it appears that this program would have little effect on racial segregation. Finally, the table shows that students who were offered vouchers reported attending schools with less fighting among students and less truancy and that parents were in closer contact with their child's teacher. Overall, it appears that students who were offered a voucher attended better schools. The results in columns (3) and (4) suggest that the effects for students who actually used a voucher were similar.

The effects of vouchers on student achievement (the national percentile ranks on combined math and reading tests) from all three experiments, as analyzed by William Howell and Paul Peterson, are reported in Table 2.3.[28] Overall, they report no effect among all students and no effect among non-African American students from attending a private school (in fact, the point estimates for non-African Americans are negative). In contrast, they find that among African American students who actually attended a private school there was an overall increase of 6.6 percentile points after three years. This result is entirely driven by the results in New York City, however, as there was no effect from switching to a private school in Washington, DC (and they only collected data in Dayton for two years)

These results — which received much attention in both the press and among policymakers — appear encouraging along several dimensions. Voucher parents were more satisfied with their children's schools, and there is evidence that the achievement of African American students offered vouchers may have increased as well. However, there are good reasons to suspect that the results reported by Howell and Peterson overstate the effect of vouchers for African American students. First, these results are only from the third year of the program; over time the effects may become even stronger or may diminish. This was evidenced by the fact that in Washington, D.C., there was a large, statistically significant effect after two years that disappeared after three years. Second, as with many longitudinal studies, there was greater attrition among the study participants not selected for a voucher than among those who were selected. The analysts attempted to compensate for this attrition using an elaborate weighting scheme; however, it is difficult to address issues regarding study participants' unobservable characteristics (such as motivation or parental support for education) using observable measures (such as test scores).

Third, it is unclear why there was an effect for African Americans but not for other groups. One explanation is that the public schools attended by the African American students in the control group were particularly bad. If so, the voucher program had its biggest effect on those who needed it most. However, it is unclear why there would have been benefits for African Americans but not for other low-income students (such as Latinos) who also attended poor performing schools. Further, Mayer and his colleagues report that in New York City (the only evaluation that presents disaggregated results) the average effect for African Americans is driven by an unusually large effect for students in the seventh grade (and a smaller effect for those in the sixth grade). There was no positive effect for African American students in grades four and five. These differences by grade level might reflect statistical variation, so that the true effect is best illustrated by the average estimate, or they might reflect something unusual about the seventh graders, so that the true effect for African Americans is exaggerated with these data.

In an attempt to probe these results further, Alan Krueger and Pei Zhu obtained the data for New York City from Mathematica Policy Research and conducted their own, independent analysis.[29] They highlight two potential problems with the Howell and Peterson analysis (as well as that by Mayer and his colleagues). First, although follow-up data were collected on students who were originally in kindergarten, these students had not been administered baseline test scores. A small fraction of the students initially in grades one through four were also missing baseline test scores. Because the experiment was conducted by randomly assigning students to receive a voucher or not, in principle one does not need to control for baseline characteristics (including test scores) since, on average, there are no differences between the students who were offered vouchers and those who were not. If one includes those missing baseline test scores in the analysis, the sample size increases by 44 percent.

Second, Howell and Peterson note that there were effects for African

Americans but not for others. As a result, the definition of who was an African American is potentially critical to the analysis. While in most data sets the individual in question self-identifies his or her race/ethnicity, in these data the researchers used the race/ethnicity of the mother to determine the race/ethnicity of the child, despite the fact that a large fraction of those who have an African American father but a mother of another race/ethnicity probably would have self-identified as African American. Therefore, Krueger and Zhu broadened the identification of African Americans to include those whose father is African American. Their results are presented in Table 2.5 along with similar results reported by Mathematica Policy Research.[30] Clearly, with the larger sample and the broader classification of who is African American, one no longer finds that there was an improvement in the achievement of African American students who were offered a voucher or who attended a private school.

As the larger sample (i.e., including those with baseline test scores) is mostly responsible for Krueger and Zhu's smaller estimated effect of the voucher program for African Americans, the results reported by Howell and Peterson and by Krueger and Zhu are not necessarily contradictory. Specifically, the effect of school vouchers may be larger for older students. However, one cannot test this hypothesis with the data from New York City alone.[31]

Because the programs in Dayton, New York City, and Washington, D.C., were privately funded, they did not necessarily incorporate the design that would likely characterize a publicly funded program.[32] As a result, researchers have also used non-experimental methods to assess whether attending a private school improves the achievement of the students who use publicly funded vouchers. Some of this evidence comes from the Milwaukee Parental Choice Program.[33]

The Milwaukee Parental Choice Program

Background and Previous Literature [34]
In 1990, Wisconsin became the first state in the nation to implement a publicly funded school voucher program. The Milwaukee Parental Choice Program provides a voucher, worth approximately $4,373 in 1996-1997, to low-income students to attend nonsectarian private schools.[35] The program began with seven private schools; by 1996 twenty schools were participating.[36] (Originally, and at the time the data were collected, religious schools were not permitted to partici-

pate in the program; they are able to do so now.) In 1996-97, the participating private schools represented a variety of educational approaches, including Montessori and Waldorf as well as bilingual and African American cultural emphases.[37] Although the tuition charged by many of the Choice schools was quite low (ranging from less than $200 to about $4,000), actual expenditures per pupil were generally higher (on the order of $4,000-$5,000 per pupil in 1996-97).[38] The balance of the revenues came from grants, donations, and fund raising by parents. Because the schools were nonsectarian, many also received Title I funding from the federal government.

Table 2.4 shows the characteristics of students who applied to the Choice program (by whether or not they were selected) and those in the Milwaukee public school sample (a random sample of students from the city's school system) who did not apply.[39] As the program is targeted at the most disadvantaged public school students, only students whose family income is at or below 1.75 times the national poverty line are eligible. In principle, a family of three with an income of approximately $21,000 (the approximate threshold during the first four years of the program) was eligible to apply; in practice, the mean family income of applicants during this time was approximately $12,300. The Choice applicants were considerably more disadvantaged than the average student in the Milwaukee public schools (whose average family income was about $24,000). Choice applicants were also more likely to be minority and to have lower pre-application math and reading test scores than the average Milwaukee public school student. On the other hand, the parental education of choice applicants was comparable to that of non-applicants.

There is considerable heterogeneity in the Milwaukee public school district, which consists of approximately 145 schools; of these, approximately 30 are "city-wide" (or magnet) schools, which were created in the 1970s to facilitate desegregation. Many of the city-wide schools are specialized, providing foreign language immersion, gifted and talented and performing arts instruction, and Montessori, Waldorf, and Global Learning educational approaches. Approximately 22 percent of the students enrolled in Milwaukee public schools are in city-wide schools.[40] Finally, a group of 14 Project Rise Schools that are predominately minority and extremely disadvantaged were exempted from desegregation. Instead, they were provided with extra funding from the state. Today, these 14 schools, along with 9 others, participate in the Preschool to Grade 5 Grant Program. Known as "P-5 schools," they enroll about 15 percent of the total public school students and 25 percent of the elementary school students. The P-5 program provides supplemental state grants to schools with high proportions of economically disadvantaged and low-achieving students. In theory, eligible schools are required to maintain pupil-teacher ratios under 25, institute annual testing in basic skills, identify students needing remedial education, increase parental involvement, provide in-service training, and conduct staff evaluations.[41] In practice, the schools primarily comply with the small class size requirement. In 1993-94, the state allocated $6.7 million to the P-5 schools; this amounted to a grant of approximately $500 per child.[42]

There are three main evaluations of the achievement effects of the Milwaukee Parental Choice Program through 1994. The first, conducted by Witte and his colleagues, concluded that there were no relative achievement gains among the Choice students.[43] The second, by Jay Greene and his colleagues, found that, by their third and fourth years in the program, the Choice students made statistically significant test score gains in both reading and math.[44] The third study, by this author, found that the students selected to attend a Choice school experienced significantly faster gains in math scores but showed no differential gains in reading.[45]

Results for African American and Hispanic Students. More than 90 percent of the participants in the Milwaukee Parental Choice Program are minority students. In order to estimate the effects of the program separately for African Americans and Hispanics, I estimated the effect of the total number of years the student has been continuously enrolled, or had ever been enrolled, in each type of school.[46] Thus, I estimate the gap in test scores between students in regular Milwaukee public schools and those enrolled in Choice, city-wide, and P-5 schools. I control for family background and student ability by including "individual fixed-effects." (See Table 2.6 for resulting fixed-effects estimates.)

With an individual fixed-effects methodology, one is able to control for all student characteristics (both observed and unobserved) that do not change over time (i.e., they are "fixed" or "time-invariant"). This includes characteristics such as degree of parental motivation, parental education, and what some call "innate" student ability. The primary disadvantage of this strategy is that it does not control for student characteristics that vary over time (e.g., changing family circumstances, health status.)

To understand this strategy, consider two students: Student A, who enrolled in a Choice school, and Student B, who did not. The panels in Figure 2.4 describe two possible test score trajectories for the two students before Student A enrolled in the Choice program.[47] Suppose that the pre-Choice test scores of Student A and Student B evolved as described in Panel A. In this panel, Student A scored higher than Student B in each of the years before Student A enrolled in the program. This may reflect that Student A was more able than Student B, and one could not attribute the test score difference to the Choice schools because they existed even before Student A enrolled in the Choice program, and they would likely have continued to exist even if Student A had remained in a Milwaukee public school. Fortunately, the fixed-effects analysis will recover the true ("unbiased," in statistical terms) effect of the Choice schools on student achievement.

The fixed-effects analysis will, however, lead to an overstatement of the program if Student A had faster test score gains than Student B before Student A enrolled in the Choice program. In this case (shown in Panel B), the fixed-effects analysis will attribute the faster achievement growth to the Choice program when, in reality, the student in the Choice program would have had faster test score growth even if he or she had remained in the Milwaukee public schools. After assessing the severity of this potential problem by analyzing the pre-application test score trajectories of students in the Choice program and those in Milwaukee public schools, I concluded that the results using individual fixed-effects are probably not overstated.[48]

Figure 2.5 shows the test scores for African American students.[49] The graph shows the *difference* in test scores between students enrolled in the regular public schools and those enrolled in Choice, city-wide, and P-5 schools. Panel A shows the math test scores, and Panel B shows the reading scores. Consider the results for math. These figures suggest that until they had been enrolled for five years in the city-wide schools, African American students scored no differently than African American students in the regular public schools. In contrast, the math scores of students in the Choice schools increased at a rate of about 2 percentile points per year, roughly the same rate of increase as those of students in the P-5 schools.

Panel B in Figure 2.5 shows the results for reading. African American students in the city-wide and Choice schools did not have faster reading test score gains than students in the regular public schools. In contrast, students in the

P-5 schools had substantially faster gains in reading than those in the other public and Choice schools. These results are very similar to those I reported in 1998, which is not surprising given that more than 50 percent of the Milwaukee public school students and about 70 percent of Choice students are African American.[50]

The results for Hispanics, in Figure 2.6, are slightly different. In particular, in math, Hispanic students in the Choice schools gained an additional 4 percentile points over students in the regular public schools; while students in the P-5 schools gained an additional 1.7 percentile points, the difference was only statistically significant at the 10 percent level. Furthermore, in contrast to the results reported in Rouse, only students in the Choice schools showed significant gains in their reading scores compared to those in the regular public schools.[51]

Overall, these results indicate that African American students in the P-5 schools had math score gains equal to those of students in the Choice schools, and reading score gains that were greater. After four years, the P-5 and Choice test score advantage was about 0.35-0.46 of a standard deviation for math; the P-5 advantage in reading was about 0.42 of a standard deviation.[52] The effect of the P-5 schools was more mixed for Hispanics, although there were gains in the choice schools. For example, among Hispanic students, after four years the math test score advantage was 0.49 (in the P-5 schools) and 0.56 (in the Choice schools) of a standard deviation; only the Hispanic students in the Choice schools showed significant increases in reading (0.4 of a standard deviation).

What might explain the fact that the P-5 and Choice schools generally outperformed the other public schools? While there are undoubtedly many factors that might explain this result, one relatively easily observed characteristic both P-5 and Choice schools had in common was a small pupil-teacher ratio, which is often used as a proxy for class size.[53,54] The average pupil-teacher ratio in the P-5 schools was 17 students per teacher; the average pupil-teacher in the Choice schools was 15.3. Both are significantly smaller than the pupil-teacher ratios in the regular and city-wide public schools. These results suggest that lower pupil-teacher ratios (or class sizes) *may* explain the differential gains by students in the Choice schools, but they do not prove that low pupil-teacher ratios explain either achievement differences between the public and private schools or between the P-5 and regular public schools.

CONCLUSION

The results from the studies reported here suggest that class size does matter and that parents who receive a voucher to enroll their child in a private school are more satisfied with the school. The evidence on whether the achievement of some of the children who use vouchers improves is mixed as well. Because the private schools in the Milwaukee Parental Choice Program and the randomized experiments had significantly smaller class sizes than the comparison public schools, it is possible that the reported school voucher results can also be explained by differences in school quality that may not derive from competitive forces. It is important to emphasize, however, that the existing voucher programs (including the randomized experiments) are too small to provide insight into the potential systemic effects of vouchers, such as the effect on students who remain in the public schools.

As a result, we know relatively little about the achievement of students who are eligible for vouchers but remain in the public schools — arguably a more important, but even more difficult, question to study. A randomized experiment designed to address this question would entail randomly dividing a group of school districts into those in which students are eligible for a voucher (the treatment group) and those in which students are not eligible (the control group). Again, after a period of time, one could infer that any achievement differences (or changes in the schools) are a result of the voucher program because, on average, the districts were similar before the program began.

This experiment has never been conducted. To date, we know little about the effects of school voucher programs on the students who are either ineligible to receive a voucher or opt to remain in their local public school despite their eligibility.[55] If Florida's Opportunity Scholarships Program survives and grows to scale, it may provide an excellent opportunity to study the effects of a publicly funded voucher program on public schools and the students who remain behind.

Finally, the research presented here suggests that we must develop a much better understanding of what makes schools effective. The class size effects from project STAR differed across schools and so did the results in Milwaukee. And yet we have little understanding of why they did. Both qualitative and quantitative research methodologies in which the characteristics (e.g., curriculum, teaching practices, school organization, class sizes) of effective schools and ineffective schools are compared would contribute greatly to the literature. If we really want to improve our educational system and prepare America's minority youth for the 21st century, it is critical that we have a better understanding of what makes good schools effective.

* * *

The author is grateful to Sue Stockly and Cecilia Conrad for their comments on this paper.

FIGURE 2.1
AVERAGE NAEP READING PROFICIENCY BY AGE
AND BY RACE/ETHNICITY, 1970-1999

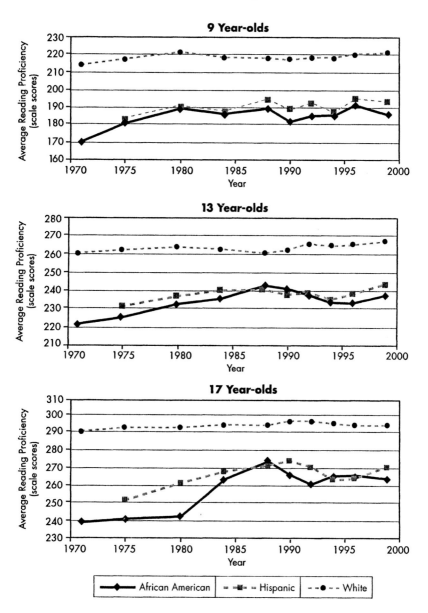

Source: *National Center for Education Statistics and* The Condition of Education, *1998.*

FIGURE 2.2

AVERAGE NAEP MATHEMATICS PROFICIENCY BY AGE AND BY RACE/ETHNICITY, 1971-1999

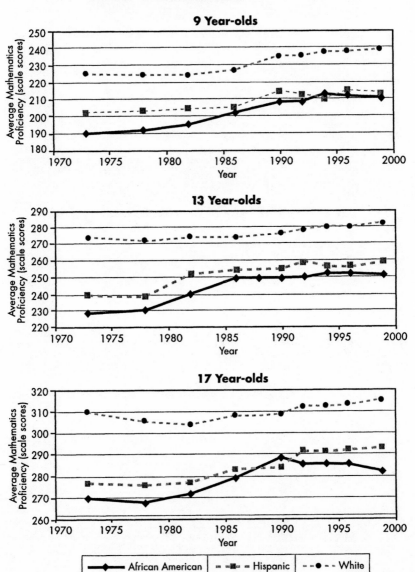

Source: National Center for Education Statistics and The Condition of Education, *1998.*

FIGURE 2.3
THE PERCENTAGE OF STUDENTS WHO
TOOK THE ACT OR SAT COLLEGE EXAM
BY INITIAL CLASS TYPE

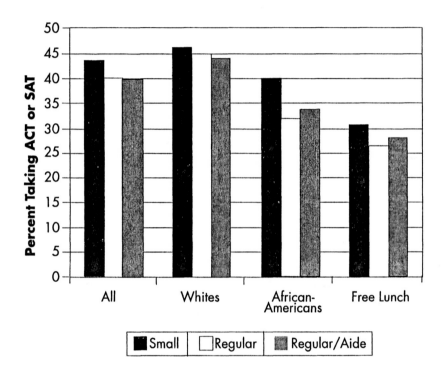

FIGURE 2.4

UNDERSTANDING INDIVIDUAL FIXED-EFFECTS

Student A is enrolled in a choice school and Student B is enrolled in a Milwaukee public school. Consider their test scores before Student a enrolled in the choice program.

Panel A. *Individual fixed effects will be generate the true effect if both Student A and B had the same growth in test scores before Student A enrolled in the choice program.*

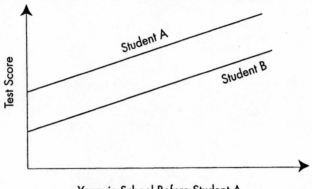

Years in School Before Student A
Enrolled in the Choice Program

Panel B. *Individual Fixed effects will overstate the effect if Student A had faster test score gains even before she enrolled in the choice program.*

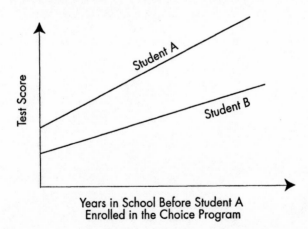

Years in School Before Student A
Enrolled in the Choice Program

FIGURE 2.5

THE DIFFERENCE IN MATH TEST SCORES BETWEEN
CHOICE, CITY-WIDE, P-5 SCHOOLS AND
"REGULAR" MILWAUKEE PUBLIC SCHOOLS

AFRICAN AMERICAN STUDENTS

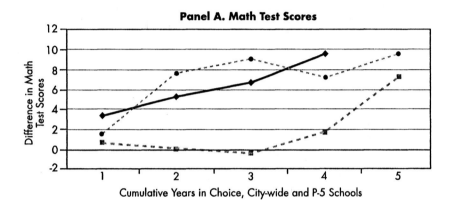

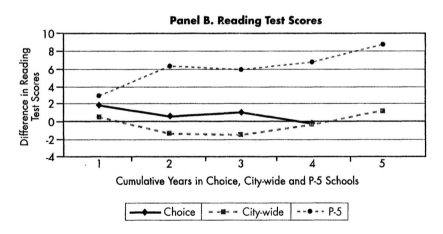

FIGURE 2.6

THE DIFFERENCE IN MATH TEST SCORES BETWEEN CHOICE, CITY-WIDE, P-5 SCHOOLS AND "REGULAR" MILWAUKEE PUBLIC SCHOOLS

HISPANIC STUDENTS

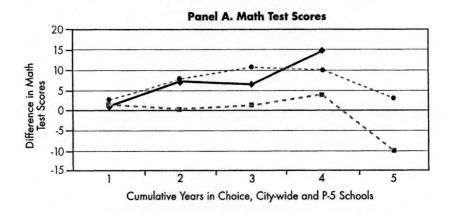

Panel A. Math Test Scores

Difference in Math Test Scores

Cumulative Years in Choice, City-wide and P-5 Schools

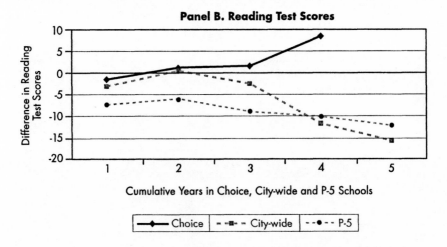

Panel B. Reading Test Scores

Difference in Reading Test Scores

Cumulative Years in Choice, City-wide and P-5 Schools

◆— Choice   – ▪ – City-wide   – ● – P-5

TABLE 2.1
THE EFFECT OF SMALL CLASS SIZES ON STUDENT ACHIEVEMENT:
EVIDENCE FROM THE TENNESSEE STAR EXPERIMENT

			Subsample		
	All Students	Free Lunch	Not on Free Lunch	Black	White
Small class	2.99	3.14	2.85	3.84	2.58
	(0.80)	(1.10)	(1.12)	(1.29)	(1.02)
Cumulative years	0.65	0.94	0.55	1.04	0.66
in small class	(0.39)	(0.59)	(0.51)	(0.68)	(0.48)
Sample size	24,349	12,064	12,285	8,150	16,069

Notes: Standard errors are in parentheses. Dependent variable is the average percentile ranking on the Stanford Achievement Test. Other covariates include whether the student was initially assigned to a regular-sized class with a teacher's aide and the cumulative number of years in such a class; the fraction of classmates in the student's class in previous year; the average fraction of classmates together in previous year; the fraction of classmates on a free lunch; the fraction of classmates who attended kindergarten; the student's gender, race and free lunch status (excluded where appropriate); and the teacher's race, gender, experience, and educational attainment.

Source: Alan Krueger, "Experimental Estimates of Education Production Fuctions," Tables IX and X.

TABLE 2.2

**THE EFFECT OF RANDOMIZED SCHOOL VOUCHERS
ON SCHOOL QUALITY
EVIDENCE FROM THE NEW YORK CITY SCHOOL CHOICE
SCHOLARSHIPS PROGRAM**

	Offered Scholarship (1)	Scholarship Offer Effect (2)	Scholarship User (3)	Private School Effect (4)
Average school size	409	-84**	382	-137
Average class size	24	-1**	26	-2**
Special program for non-English Speakers	55	-22**	49	-40**
Special programs for learning disabled	70	-8**	68	-14**
Special programs for advanced learners	54	-4	51	-7
Computer Laboratory	91	7**	93	12**
Percentage of students in child's class is of the same race/ethnic background as this child?				
Less than 25 percent	19	2	16	3
25-50 percent	20	2	19	4
50-75 percent	20	-5*	28	-8*
More than 75 percent but not all	28	-3	33	-5*
Everyone	12	3*	33	5*
Parents report fighting is a serious problem in school	44	-18**	34	-30**
Parents report students missing class a serious problem in school	37	-15**	30	-25**
Child has more than 1 hour of Homework	57	15**	63	26**
Parents participate in instruction	65	12**	67	20**
Parents receive notes from teacher	90	10**	93	17**
Parent very satisfied with academic Quality	37	20**	48	34**

Notes: Statistically significant at the 5% level in a two-tailed test. ** Statistically significant at the 1% level in a two-tailed test. The "Scholarship offer effect" estimates the impact of having been offered a scholarship. The "Private School Effect" estimates the impact of attending a private school using two-stage least squares.

Source: Daniel Mayer, Paul Peterson, David Meyers, Christina Clark Tuttle, and William Howell, School Choice in New York City After Three Years: An Evaluation of the School Choice Scholarships Program (Mathematica Policy Research Inc., 2002).

TABLE 2.3

THE EFFECT OF RANDOMIZED SCHOOL VOUCHERS ON STUDENT ACHIEVEMENT: EVIDENCE FROM THE DAYTON OH, NEW YORK AND WASHINGTON DC SCHOOL CHOICE SCHOLARSHIPS PROGRAM

	Year 1 Scholarship Offer Effect (1)	Year 2 Scholarship Offer Effect (2)	Year 3 Private School Effect (3)
All Students			
Dayton, OH	2.2	4.2	NA
New York City	1.1	0.6	1.4
Washington, DC	-0.3	7.5**	-2.1
All three cities	0.7	3.7	0.7
African-Americans Students			
Dayton, OH	3.3	6.5	NA
New York City	5.4**	4.3*	8.9**
Washington, DC	-0.9	9.2**	-1.9
All three cities	3.9	6.3*	6.6*
Students From All Other Ethnic Groups			
Dayton, OH	1.0	-0.2	NA
New York City	-2.2	-1.5	-3.3
Washington, DC	7.4	-0.1	-1.8
All three cities	-1.0	-1.4	-3.5

Notes:* Statistically significant at the 5% level in a two-tailed test; ** statistically significant at the 1% level in a two-tailed test. The dependent variable is the combined math and reading test scores (reported in national percentile ranks). The "Private school effect" estimates the impact of attending a private school using two-stage-least squares. Data were only collected in Dayton, OH for two years.

Source: William Howell and Paul Peterson, The Education Gap: Vouchers and Urban Schools (Washington, DC: The Brookings Institution Press, 2002).

TABLE 2.4

**MEAN CHARACTERISTICS OF APPLICANTS TO
THE CHOICE PROGRAM AND STUDENTS
IN THE MILWAUKEE PUBLIC SCHOOLS**

| | APPLICANTS | | Milwaukee Public |
	Selected	Not Selected	School Sample
African American	0.721	0.780	0.550
	(0.011)	(0.012)	(0.007)
Hispanic	0.217	0.154	0.097
	(0.011)	(0.011)	(0.004)
Pre-application math score	34.560	35.073	43.353
(national percentile ranking)	(1.196)	(1.552)	(0.494)
Pre-application reading score	33.869	34.341	40.227
(national percentile ranking)	(1.050)	(1.369)	(0.462)
Family income (Π 1000)	$12,123	$12,715	$23,897
(1994 dollars)	(0.297)	(0.509)	(0.534)
Mother's education	12.559	12.399	12.108
	(0.067)	(0.109)	(0.055)
Father's education	12.048	11.521	12.250
	(0.092)	(0.152)	(0.068)
Maximum number	1,544	1,219	5,318
of observations			

Notes: Standard errors are in parentheses.

Source: Cecilia Rouse, "Private School Vouchers and Student Achievement" (1998), Table I.

TABLE 2.5

THE EFFECT OF RANDOMIZED SCHOOL VOUCHERS ON STUDENT ACHIEVEMENT AFTER THREE YEARS: EVIDENCE FROM THE NEW YORK CITY SCHOOL CHOICE SCHOLARSHIP PROGRAM

	Year 1 Scholarship Offer Effect (1)	Year 3 Private School Effect (2)
All Students		
Mayer et al.	0.9	1.3
Krueger and Zhu	-0.04	-0.1
African-Americans Students		
Mayer, et al	5.5**	7.5**
Krueger and Zhu	1.5	2.2
Latino Students		
Mayer, et al	-0.9	-1.4
Krueger and Zhu	-0.4	-0.6

Notes: * Statistically significant at the 5% level in a two-tailed test.

** Statistically significant at the 1% level in a two-tailed test. The dependent variable is the combined math and reading test scores (reported in national percentile ranks). The "Scholarship offer effect" estimates the impact of having been offered a scholarship. The "Private school effect" estimates the impact of attending a private school using two-stage-least squares.

Sources: Mayer et al., "School Choice in New York City After Three Years," Table 20; and Alan Krueger and Pei Zhu, "Another Look at the New York City School Voucher Experiment" (American Behavioral Scientist, 2003 [forthcoming]).

TABLE 2.6

INDIVIDUAL FIXED-EFFECT (FE) ESTIMATES OF THE EFFECT OF CHOICE SCHOOLS, CITY-WIDE, AND P-5 SCHOOLS ON MATH AND READING TEST SCORES FOR AFRICAN AMERICAN AND HISPANIC STUDENTS

| | African American Students | | Hispanic Students | |
	Math	Reading	Math	Reading
Currently enrolled in city-wide school	0.069 (1.331)	-0.519 (1.234)	1.645 (2.620)	-5.286 (2.397)
Enrolled in city-wide school 1 year	0.654 (1.658)	0.885 (1.535)	-0.110 (3.297)	2.123 (3.027)
Enrolled in city-wide school 2 years	-0.011 (1.759)	-0.832 (1.664)	-1.385 (3.577)	5.648 (3.268)
Enrolled in city-wide school 3 years	-0.376 (1.933)	-1.010 (1.793)	-0.473 (4.179)	2.802 (3.882)
Enrolled in city-wide school 4 years	1.711 (2.392)	0.271 (2.211)	2.146 (5.782)	-6.336 (5.264)
Enrolled in city-wide school 5 years	7.274 (3.449)	1.668 (2.995)	-11.375 (14.104)	-10.497 (13.036)
Currently enrolled in P-5 School	1.532 (0.808)	0.540 (0.758)	0.551 (2.057)	-5.097 (1.892)
Enrolled in P-5 school 1 year	0.079 (2.060)	2.369 (1.920)	2.072 (5.869)	-2.127 (5.138)
Enrolled in P-5 school 2 years	6.171 (2.106)	5.832 (1.953)	7.214 (6.052)	-0.812 (5.336)
Enrolled in P-5 school 3 years	7.557 (2.266)	5.378 (2.099)	10.261 (6.294)	-3.744 (5.556)
Enrolled in P-5 school 4 years	5.738 (2.482)	6.244 (2.306)	9.651 (6.616)	-4.909 (5.879)
Enrolled in P-5 school 5 years	8.045 (2.866)	8.378 (2.672)	2.559 (7.377)	-6.947 (6.624)
Currently enrolled in Choice school	-2.102 (1.548)	-2.181 (1.480)	-9.354 (3.823)	-4.199 (3.404)
Enrolled in Choice school 1 year	5.524 (1.999)	3.988 (1.889)	10.301 (4.667)	2.614 (4.228)
Enrolled in Choice school 2 years	7.415 (2.108)	2.771 (1.991)	16.720 (4.919)	5.439 (4.424)
Enrolled in Choice school 3 years	8.820 (2.353)	3.216 (2.225)	15.925 (5.465)	5.754 (4.969)
Enrolled in Choice school 4 years	11.716 (2.902)	2.052 (2.730)	24.180 (10.309)	12.591 (9.489)
R2	0.775	0.746	0.828	0.805
Number of observations	6822	6836	1218	1225

Notes: Standard errors are in parentheses. All specifications also include a constant and dummy variables indicating the grade level of the student when her or she took the test. The math score regressions include a dummy variable indicating if the test score was imputed. "Enrolled" is the total number of years the student has continuously been enrolled, or had ever been enrolled, in the particular type of school. All specifications include individual fixed-effects.

Source: Author's calculations.

NOTES

1. John Wirt, Tom Snyder, Jennifer Sable, Susan P. Choy, Yupin Bae, Janis Stennet, Allison Gruner, and Marianne Perie, *The Condition of Education, 1998* (NCES 98-013) (Washington, D.C.: U.S. Department of Education, National Center for Education Statistics: 1998).

2. Richard J. Murnane, John B. Willet, and Frank Levy, "The Growing Importance of Cognitive Skills in Wage Determination," *Review of Economics and Statistics* 77, no. 2 (May 1995): 251-266.

3. Whole-school reforms are based on the theory that changing only a single aspect of the educational process is inadequate; only comprehensive change will make a difference. As a result, many of these models emphasize the formulation of a common school vision, and address, in some way, school organization, professional development, curriculum, and instruction. Examples of such models include the Accelerated Schools Project, the Edison Project, the Modern Red Schoolhouse, Roots & Wings, and Success for All. These models are currently operating in thousands of schools in all states in the nation (Northwest Regional Educational Laboratory, *Catalog of School Reform Models: First Edition* [March 1998]).

4. Charter schools have been gaining in popularity since the early 1990s. As with vouchers, this reform is an attempt to create more competitive pressure and schooling alternatives, although only from within the existing public school system. Generally, charter schools have a contract with the state or the school district that specifies the terms of their operation and obligations in order to receive state funds. And as long as the schools meet pre-established accountability goals, they have more autonomy than public schools in decisions about staffing, curriculum, and school organization (U.S. Department of Education, "A Study of Charter Schools: A First Year Report," http://wws.ed.gov/pubs/charter [May 1997]).

5. At this time, there are ongoing large-scale evaluations of both reforms.

6. Test scores are often used to measure short-run outcomes for schooling because they can be administered fairly frequently and at relatively low cost. However, they are not necessarily good indicators of long-run outcomes, such as eventual educational attainment and labor market success.

7. The achievement levels in writing have been more nearly constant for all groups; the achievement gains in science more closely resemble those in math and reading although with more variability (Wirt et al., *The Condition of Education*). These trends are also evident among disadvantaged urban students (Alan B. Krueger, "Reassessing the View That American Schools Are Broken," *Economic Policy Review* 4, no. 1 [March 1998]: 29-46.).

8. Wirt et al., *The Condition of Education*; Eric A. Hanushek, "Conclusions and Controversies About the Effectiveness of School Resources," *Economic Policy Review* 4, no. 1 (March 1998): 11-27.

9. Hanushek, "Conclusions and Controversies."

10. Krueger, "Reassessing the View."

11. Two recent papers on this topic use quasi-experimental designs: Joshua Angrist and Victor Lavy ("Using Maimonides' Rule to Estimate the Effect of Class Size on Children's Academic Achievement," *Quarterly Journal of Economics* 114, no. 2 [May 1999]: 533-575) use the nonlinearity in the class size determination in Israel to identify an effect of class size and find effects on the same order of magnitude as those reported by Alan B. Krueger ("Experimental Estimates of Education Production Functions," *Quarterly Journal of*

Economics 114, no. 2 [May 1999]: 497-531); and Caroline M. Hoxby ("The Effects of Class Size and Composition on Student Achievement: New Evidence from Natural Population Variation," *Quarterly Journal of Economics* 128, no. 4 [2000]: 1239-1285) exploits variation in the size of the school-aged population in Connecticut to identify an effect of class size and finds that small class sizes have no effect on student achievement.

12. Krueger, "Experimental Estimates of Education Production Functions." Note that since each child is in the evaluation for more than one year, the sample size in the analysis is 24,349.

13. For previous evaluations, see Elizabeth Word, J. Johnston, Helen Bain, et al., "The State of Tennessee's Student/Teacher Achievement Ratio (STAR) Project: Technical Report 1985-1990" (Nashville: Tennessee State Department of Education, 1990); Jeremy D. Finn and Charles M. Achilles, "Answers and Questions About Class Size: A Statewide Experiment," *American Educational Research Journal* 27, no. 3 (Fall 1990): 557-577; and John Folger and Carolyn Breda, "Evidence from Project STAR About Class Size and Student Achievement," *Peabody Journal of Education*, vol. 67 (1989), pp. 17-33.

14. Krueger, "Experimental Estimates," Tables IX and X.

15. Alan B. Krueger and Diane M. Whitmore, "The Effect of Attending a Small Class in the Early Grades on College Test Taking and Middle School Test Results: Evidence from Project STAR," *Economic Journal*, vol. 111 (January 2001): pp. 1-28..

16. Brian M. Stecher and George W. Bohrnstedt, "Class Size Reduction in California: Early Evaluation Findings, 1996-98," CSR Research Consortium Technical Report (June 1999); Edward Wexler, JoAnn Izu, Lisa Carlos, Bruce Fuller, Gerald Hayward, and Mike Kirst, "California's Class Size Reduction: Implications for Equity, Practice, and Implementation," WestEd Technical Report (March 1998).

17. Stecher and Bohrnstedt, "Class Size Reduction in California."

18. These figures are updated estimates based on Krueger ("Experimental Estimates"); the expenditure figures are from the *Digest of Education Statistics 1998* (DOE, National Center for Education Statistics [1998], http://nces.ed.gov/pubs99/digest98). In California, costs to reduce class size have ranged from $0 to $1,000 per student, depending on how far the district was from the target of 20 students per class (Wexler et al., "California's Class Size Reduction").

19. Krueger, "Experimental Estimates."

20. John E. Chubb and Terry M. Moe, *Politics, Markets, and America's Schools* (Washington, DC: The Brookings Institution, 1990); and Milton Friedman, *Capitalism and Freedom* (Chicago: University of Chicago Press, 1962).

21. See, for example, Lisa Barrow and Cecilia Elena Rouse, "Using Market Valuation to Assess Public School Spending," National Bureau of Economic Research Working paper No. 9054 (Princeton University, July 2002): Melvin V. Borland and Roy M. Howsen, "Student Academic Achievement and the Degree of Market Concentration in Education," *Economics of Education Review* 11, no. 1 (1992): 31-39; and Caroline Minter Hoxby, "The Effects of Private School Vouchers on Schools and Students" in *Holding Schooling Accountable: Performance-Based Reform in Education*, ed. Helen F. Ladd (Washington, DC: The Brookings Institution, 1996); "The Effects of Class Size and Composition"; and "Does Competition Among Public Schools Benefit Students and Taxpayers? Evidence from National Variation in School Districting," *American Economic Review* 90, no. 5 (December 2000): 1209-1238.

22. See, for example, Carl Bagley, Philip Woods, and Ron Glatter, "Barriers to School Responsiveness in the Education Quasi-Market," *School Organisation* 16, no. 1 (1996): 45-58; Donald E. Frey, "Can Privatizing Education Really Improve Achievement? An Essay Review," *Economics of Education Review* 11, no. 4 (1992): 427-438; and W.T. Garner and Jane Hannaway, "Private Schools: The Client Connection," in *Family Choice in Schooling*, ed. M. Manley-Casimir (Lexington, MA: D.C. Heath, 1982).

23. The voucher does not cover the full tuition for most of the voucher students. After the first year, the most cited source for additional funds was family income (34 percent), followed by a school scholarship (22 percent). Other sources included funding from relatives and friends and tuition reductions in exchange for donating time and fund-raising support (Paul E. Peterson, David Myers, and William G. Howell, "An Evaluation of the New York City School Choice Scholarships Program: The First Year," Harvard University Program on Education Policy and Governance, Working Paper PEPG 98-12 (1998)).

24. Daniel P. Mayer, Paul Peterson, David E. Myers, Christina Clark Tuttle, and William G. Howell, "School Choice in New York City After Three Years: An Evaluation of the School Choice Scholarships Program," Mathematica Policy Research Inc. Final Report (February 2002).

25. J. Angrist, G. Imbens, and D. Rubin, "Identification of Causal Effects Using Instrumental Variables," *Journal of the American Statistical Association* 91, no. 434 (1996): 444-455; James Heckman and Jeffrey Smith, "Assessing the Case for Randomized Evaluation of Social Programs," in *Measuring Labour Market Measures: Evaluating the Effects of Active Labour Market Policies*, ed. Karsten Jensen and Per Kongshoj (Copenhagen: Ministry of Labour, 1993).

26. Mayer et al., "School Choice in New York City After Three years."

27. Note, however, that these results, per se, do not *prove* that the private schools do not admit students with special needs; private schools may enroll students needing compensatory education but not provide special classes for them.

28. William G. Howell and Paul B. Peterson, with Patrick J. Wolf and David E. Campbell, *The Education Gap: Vouchers and Urban Schools* (Washington, DC: The Brookings Institution Press, 2002).

29. Alan B. Krueger and Pei Zhu, "Another Look at the New York City School Voucher Experiment," *American Behavioral Scientist*, 2003 (forthcoming).

30. Mayer et al., "School Choice in New York City After Three Years." The estimates for the effect of private schools in Table 2.5 are not strictly comparable to those in Table 2.3. Namely, the estimates in Table 2.3 reflect the effect for students who remained in the private schools for the specified period of time (1, 2 or 3 years); the estimates in Table 2.5 reflect the effect for students who ever enrolled in a private school. The Mayer et al results are presented as they are, in principle, based on the same data and analysis as those presented by Howell et al.

31. One could test this hypothesis by comparing data across the three cities. That said, it is unclear why, if the effect is larger for older students, one does not observe such a pattern among Latino students.

32. For example, the private schools in the privately funded programs were allowed to charge additional tuition to the scholarship students above the scholarship amount, and they were allowed to choose which students to admit— neither of which are permitted in the existing publicly funded programs.

33. In 1996, the city of Cleveland, Ohio, began a voucher program that allows students to attend any private school, including religious schools. Jay Greene and his colleagues report that the students in two of the larger participating private schools showed achievement gains over the first year of the program (Jay P. Greene, William G. Howell, and Paul E. Peterson, "An Evaluation of the Cleveland Scholarship Program," Program on Education Policy and Governance (Cambridge, MA: Harvard University, March 1997, mimeographed). They did not, however, have a control group (students who were not enrolled in private schools) with which to compare test scores.

34. Much of the material in this section is drawn from the following works by the author: "Private School Vouchers and Student Achievement: An Evaluation of the Milwaukee Parental Choice Program," *Quarterly Journal of Economics* 113, no. 2 (May 1998): 553-602; and "Schools and Student Achievement: More on the Milwaukee Parental Choice Program," *Economic Policy Review* 4, no. 1 (March 1998): 61-78.

35. For excellent descriptions of the program through 1994, see John F. Witte, Christopher A. Thorn, Kim M. Pritchard, and Michele Claibourn, "Fourth-Year Report: Milwaukee Parental Choice Program" (University of Wisconsin, December 1994, mimeographed); and John F. Witte, Troy D. Sterr, and Christopher A. Thorn, "Fifth-Year Report: Milwaukee Parental Choice Program" (University of Wisconsin, December 1995, mimeographed). The Wisconsin Department of Public Instruction also has information about the current program in *Directions: Your School Selection Guide for the 1997-98 School Year* (Milwaukee, WI: 1997).

36. Originally the private schools in the Choice program were only allowed to admit up to 49 percent of their students as part of the program; this level was raised to 65 percent in 1994. And the number of students who could participate in the Choice program was originally limited to 1 percent of the Milwaukee public school enrollment in the first four years, but was expanded to 1.5 percent in 1994. This meant that only about a thousand students could be in the program at any one time during the first four years.

37. The descriptive statistics that follow track the first four years of the program because data on student achievement are only available for this time.

38. I obtained this information by calling the five schools enrolling the largest proportion of the Choice students. Combined, these schools enrolled over 95 percent of the Choice students.

39. Rouse, "Private School Vouchers."

40. Author's calculations based on the Common Core of Data from 1991-92 (a census of public schools conducted by the National Center for Educational Statistics).

41. Dan Clancy, Charlie Toulmin, and Merry Bukolt, "Wisconsin Public School Finance Programs, 1993-94," in *Public School Finance Programs of the United States and Canada 1993-94*, ed. Steven D. Gold, David M. Smith, and Stephen B. Lawton (New York: American Education Finance Association, 1995).

42. Author's calculations based on the Common Core of Data from 1991-1992.

43. Witte, Sterr, and Thorn, "Fifth-Year Report"; see also John F. Witte, "Achievement Effects of the Milwaukee Voucher Program" (University of Wisconsin at Madison, Madison, WI: January 1997, mimeographed).

44. Jay P. Greene, Paul E. Peterson, and Jiangtao Du, "The Effectiveness of School Choice: The Milwaukee Experiment," Harvard University Education Policy and Governance Occasional Paper 97-1 (March 1997).

45. See Rouse, "Private School Vouchers" and "Schools and Student Achievement," for discussions of the methodological differences between the three studies. In addition, the results found by Greene et al. ("The Effectiveness of School Choice") and Rouse are consistent with a non-experimental literature that attempts to infer the impact of vouchers by examining the relative performance of public and private schools (e.g., Richard J. Murnane, "A Review Essay—Comparisons of Public and Private Schools: Lessons from the Uproar," *Journal of Human Resources* 19 (1984): 263-277; William N. Evans and Robert M. Schwab, "Finishing High School and Starting College: Do Catholic Schools Make a Difference?" *Quarterly Journal of Economics* 110 (November 1995): 941-974. In particular, although the overall impact of private schools is mixed, this literature suggests that Catholic schools generate higher test scores for African Americans (Derek Neal, "The Effects of Catholic Secondary Schooling on Educational Achievement," *Journal of Labor Economics* 15, no. 1, part 1 [January 1997]: 98-123; David N. Figlio and Joe A. Stone, "Are Private Schools Really Better?" *Research in Labor Economics*, vol. 18 (1999), pp. 115-140.

46. I do not present the results for whites because of small sample sizes.

47. Rouse, "Schools and Student Achievement." Another way to think about these panels is that they represent what the test score trajectories would have been for both students in the absence of the Choice program.

48. Rouse, "Private School Vouchers."

49. The underlying coefficient estimates and standard errors for Figures 2.5 and 2.6 are in Table 2.6.

50. Rouse, "Schools and Student Achievement."

51. Rouse, "Private School Vouchers"; "Schools and Student Achievement."

52. I used the national standard deviation for normal curve equivalent scores of 21 for these calculations.

53. Although highly correlated, the pupil-teacher ratio does not always directly correspond to the average class size. Rather, the two measures diverge as intraschool variation in class size increases, due for example to special and compensatory education (Michael A. Boozer and Cecilia Elena Rouse, "Intra-School Variation in Class Size: Patterns and Implications," *Journal of Urban Economics* 50, no. 1 (July 2001): pp. 163-189. To illustrate, while the average pupil-teacher ratio in the Choice schools was 15.3 students per teacher, the average class size was 23.6. Unfortunately, data on average class size for the Milwaukee public schools were not readily available.

54. The estimates of the pupil-teacher ratios for the Choice schools are based on the schools I contacted. I used the 1991-1992 Common Core of Data to estimate the pupil-teacher ratios for the public schools.

55. Mathematica Policy Research and Paul Peterson attempted a nonexperimental study of the effects of providing vouchers to all students in one school district, the Edgewood School District, in San Antonio, Texas. Paul Peterson, David Myers, and William G. Howell ("An Evaluation of the Horizon Scholarship Program in the Edgewood Independent School District, San Antonio, Texas: The First Year," Mathematica Policy Research and Program on Education Policy and Governance Working Paper [1999]) reported results that indicated

increased parental satisfaction; however, the project was terminated after one year because of a lack of cooperation from the public schools (Jay P. Greene and Daryl Hall, "The CEO Horizon Scholarship Program: A Case Study of School Vouchers in the Edgewood Independent School District, San Antonio, Texas," Mathematica Policy Research Inc., Final Report [May 2001]).

Chapter Three

THE DIGITAL DIVIDE IN EDUCATING
BLACK STUDENTS AND WORKERS

Alan B. Krueger

INTRODUCTION

As former Senator Bill Bradley has observed, the American job market is increasingly connected to information technology. In 1997, more than half of all workers directly used a computer keyboard on the job. Workers who use a computer in their daily routine are paid more than those who do not, and they are more highly sought after by employers.[1] The Commerce Department's 1999 report, *Falling Through the Net: Defining the Digital Divide,* highlighted the fact that African American families are less likely than others to have access to information technology at home and at work.[2] This chapter explores the racial divide in the use of computer technology among schoolchildren. Computers in school are used for substantive instruction (e.g., learning the times tables), to search for information, and to prepare students to use information technology once they enter the job market. The goal of my research was to measure the extent of the digital divide in computer-related training in elementary and secondary schools and to evaluate its likely consequences.

Schools can be a powerful force for bridging the divide in access to information technology; they can also reinforce existing gaps between African Americans and members of other races. The next section reviews evidence on the "racial divide" in computer use in school. The results indicate that African American schoolchildren are less likely than white students to use computers in school, although the gap narrowed considerably in the 1980s and 1990s. A

Alan Krueger is Bendheim professor of economics and public affairs at Princeton University and director of the Princeton University Survey Research Center.

10-percentage-point black-white gap in computer use remains in the elementary school grades, but in 1997 black and white high school students were equally likely to use computers in school. Black students were also less likely to use the Internet in school than were white students, and this gap was larger for high school students than for elementary and middle school students.

The second section, "Educational Consequences of the Computer Use Gap," considers evidence on the efficacy of computer technology in achieving educational goals. Despite the rapid increase in computer use at school, there is surprisingly little compelling scientific evidence documenting that computer technology raises student achievement levels. The third section, "The Job Market and Computer Literacy," reviews evidence on the possible link between computer-related skills and success in the job market. It appears that workers who have computer skills have much better job prospects than those who lack such skills. It is still an open question, however, whether employers seek out, and highly reward, workers who have computer skills because they value those skills or because computer competence is correlated with other desirable worker attributes. The conclusion offers suggestions for narrowing the digital divide.

THE DIGITAL DIVIDE IN COMPUTER USE AT SCHOOL

Several studies have documented a racial gap in information technology in schools. Some studies evaluate data on the number of computers or Internet connections in schools, disaggregated by the racial composition of the schools' students, whereas others evaluate student-level data on computer usage in school. The previous research has primarily focused on the 1980s.

Most of the previous research has found lower utilization or prevalence of computers in schools predominantly attended by black students.[3] Henry Becker analyzed data from the National Survey of School Uses of Microcomputers, conducted by the Center for Social Organization at Johns Hopkins University between December 1982 and March 1983. Becker found that students who attended a school with a high concentration of non-white students had a higher ratio of students to computers than schools with a higher proportion of white students.[4] Based on Johns Hopkins' Second National Survey of 2,331 public and private schools conducted in spring 1985, Becker and Carleton Sterling found that schools with a higher percentage of non-white students were less likely to have any computers used by students, and the gap was larger at the elementary school (K-6) level.[5] The results were similar in a third Johns Hopkins survey conducted in 1989: Schools with a high concentration of non-white children had fewer computers per student, especially in the elementary grades.[6] The 1989 survey found that elementary schools with less than one-quarter minority students had 28.6 students per computer, while schools with a majority of non-white students had 39.4 students per computer; for upper secondary schools, the corresponding ratios of students per computer were 25.6 for predominantly white schools and 24.8 for predominantly non-white schools.

When Michael Boozer, Shari Wolkon and I examined data on student use of computers in the 1984 and 1989 October Current Population Surveys (CPS), we found that black and Hispanic students were less likely than white students to use computers in school. In both 1984 and 1989, the gap was larger in elementary school grades than in middle school and high school, and by 1989 the gap for grades 9-12 had narrowed to only 4 percentage points.[7]

In a recent study, Harold Wenglinsky calculates the frequency of computer use based on data on fourth and eighth graders from the 1996 National Assessment of Educational Progress (NAEP) in mathematics, and evaluates the impact of computer use on students' math test scores.[8] The computer-use data analyzed by Wenglinsky from the NAEP questionnaire are self-reported by the students, like the CPS data. A unique advantage of the NAEP data is that they also contain teacher-reported information on the teachers' previous computer preparation, and information on the type of use of computers (e.g., simulations, applications, drills, and practice). Wenglinsky looked only at use of computers for math. In contrast to most of the previous literature, Wenglinsky found that black fourth grade students were more likely than white fourth graders to use computers at school at least once a week (42 versus 32 percent). He also found that black eighth graders were more likely than white eighth graders to use a computer at least once a week for math applications, but this differential was statistically insignificant (33 versus 28 percent). It is unclear whether peculiarities of the NAEP data generated this result, or whether black students actually were more likely to use computers in school than white students. On the basis of no direct evidence on the impact of public policy, however, Wenglinsky concluded, "It seems that policies to promote computer access in school have succeeded in eliminating inequities of this sort [access to computer technology]." On the other hand, Wenglinsky found that "Disadvantaged groups do seem to be less likely to have teachers well-prepared to use computers," and that, compared to white students, "Blacks are less likely to use computers for applications and more likely to use them for drill and practice."[9]

Table 3.1 extends the previous literature by calculating the percentage, by race and Hispanic ethnicity, of students who directly used a computer in school in selected years between 1984 and 1997. (Hispanic students can be of any race.) The table is based on data from the October CPS. In 1984, 1989, 1993, and 1997, the School Enrollment Supplement to the October CPS contained a set of questions on computer use. The main question of interest is: "Do you directly use a computer at school?" Direct use of a computer was defined as hands-on use of a computer that involved using a computer keyboard, and computers could include personal computers, laptops, mini-computers or mainframe computers.[10] Two noteworthy advantages of the CPS data are that the computer use question is consistent over time, and the data are collected for a large, nationally representative sample. A potential disadvantage of the survey data is that proxy responses were accepted; that is, one family member could respond on behalf of another. (To generate the estimates in Table 3.1, I calculated weighted percentages of students who used a computer in school, where the weights are the CPS final weights. See Appendix Tables 3a and 3b for standard errors and sample sizes for the estimates.)

The results in Table 3.1 indicate a tremendous increase in the use of computers in school since the mid-1980s. In 1984 fewer than one-third of all students reported using a computer in school, but by 1997 more than three-quarters of all students reported doing so. For students as a whole, in the years reported, computer use was more prevalent among elementary school students than high school students. Looking at all grades combined, black students were 16 percentage points less likely than white students to use a computer in school in 1984, and by 1997, the gap was only 6 points Consistent with findings in most of the previous literature, the black-white gap in this measure of computer use has historically been larger in grades 1-8 than in high school. Indeed, the figures in Table 3.1 indicate that the black-white gap in the proportion of students who used a computer in school had completely disappeared by 1997 for high school students, while a 10-point black-white gap remained for students in grades 1-8. From 1984-93 Hispanic students were more likely to use computers in school than black students, but by 1997 this gap had been reversed; there was now a Hispanic-black gap of 5 percentage points, and the Hispanic-white gap in computer use had become larger than the black-white gap.

The 1997 CPS data also contained a question on the frequency with which computers were used in school. According to these data, three-quarters of the students who used a computer at school used it every day or several times a week; only 5 percent used a computer less frequently than once a week. If we follow Wenglinsky and define computer use as using a computer at least once per week, the racial gaps that are apparent in Table 3.1 are slightly smaller, but still substantial. For example, in 1997 some 77.7 percent of white students in grades 1-8 used a computer at least once a week, compared to 68.7 percent of black students. If we look at the CPS data for fourth graders, black students were 10 percentage points less likely than white students to use a computer in school at least once a week (75 versus 85 percent); this is contrary to Wenglinsky's finding, based on the NAEP data, that black fourth graders were 10 points more likely to use a computer.

Simply using a computer is a crude measure of the extent of information technology used in schools. This measure misses the intensity with which computers are used, as well as the purpose and efficacy of computer use. The 1997 CPS asked respondents: "Do you use the INTERNET (or another on-line service) at school?" Table 3.2 reports the percentage of students from different racial backgrounds who report using the Internet in school. African American students are less likely to use the Internet than are white students. And the gap in Internet use is greatest at the high school level: 27.4 percent of white high school students use the Internet at school, compared to 19.1 percent of black students. The gap is even greater between white and Hispanic students (27.4 versus 15.9).

Differences in computer use can arise for many reasons, such as geographic location, degree of urbanization, and family income among members of different racial groups. To examine the racial gap in computer use further, Table 3.3 reports Ordinary Least Squares estimates of linear probability models using the 1984 CPS.[11] The dependent variable in these models is a dummy variable that equals one if the student uses a computer in school, and zero if he or she does not. In the first column, only race and Hispanic ethnicity are held constant. White students are the base group. In column 2, additional controls are included to hold constant the students' sex, grade, age and public or private school attendance. Column 3 further controls for the region the student resides in, city type, and city size. Finally, column 4 additionally controls for 14 dummy variables indicating ranges of the student's family income. The sample was restricted to children aged 6-18 in grades 1-12.

The regression results reported in column 1 indicate that in 1984 black students were 17 percentage points less likely than white students to use a computer in school.[12] The full set of controls included in column 4 account for almost half of the black-white gap in school-based computer use. Income and region of residence are particularly important factors in accounting for the black-white gap in computer use. Nonetheless, about a 9 point black-white gap in computer use remains after all the variables in column 4 are held constant. The effects of some of the other variables in Table 3 are also of interest: girls are slightly less likely to use computers in school than are boys; students who are in a higher grade for their age level are more likely to use computers, while students who are old for their grade are less likely to use computers; and although it is not shown in the table, students from high-income families are more likely to use computers in school than are students from low-income families.

Tables 3.4, 3.5, and 3.6 provide the corresponding regression results for data from the 1989, 1993, and 1997 October CPS. In these later years, the coefficient estimates are generally similar to those for 1984 (or at least of the same sign), although one notable change is that by the 1990s, students in the South had become more likely to use computers than those in the West. Most important for our purposes, the same pattern emerges as in the earlier data: Controlling for family income and regional characteristics accounts for almost half of the black-white gap in computer use.

What might account for the black-white gap in computer use that remains after adjusting for differences in family income, demographic characteristics, grade level, and region? Several factors could be at work. First, schools that are predominantly attended by minority students could lack resources to purchase computers, even conditional on the students' family income. Second, teachers in schools that are attended by minority children could lack the training or background to use computers. Alternatively, teachers of minority students may prefer to teach with traditional methods rather than using computers because they think such methods are more beneficial for their students. The fact that the black-white gap in computer use in school has eroded for high school students suggests that differences in teacher competencies and resources have been overcome in high schools.

A final issue concerns the use of computers at home. African American children are much less likely to live in households that own computers and therefore are less likely to use computers at home. A tabulation of the October

1997 CPS indicates that 51 percent of white students aged 6-18 directly used a computer at home, while only 21 percent of black students did so. And the black-white gap in computer use at home was greater for high school students than for elementary and middle school students. The gap in computer use was only partially accounted for by the lower average income of African American families. Tabulations from the CPS data further indicate that, among students who used a computer at home, black students were less likely than white students to use the computer for educational programs (40 versus 48 percent) or to complete school assignments (58 versus 64 percent).[13] The racial gap in computer use in school may be a partial manifestation of the gap in computer use at home: Children who are not exposed to computers at home may feel less comfortable using them in school than children who live in homes with computers.

Regardless of the source of the digital divide, at home and at school African American children are exposed to computer technology less often than white children. The next sections consider the consequences of this digital divide for academic achievement and job market success.

EDUCATIONAL CONSEQUENCES OF THE COMPUTER USE GAP

There is surprisingly little compelling evidence on the efficacy of Computer-Assisted Instruction (CAI). In part, the problem arises because technology is changing so quickly. Different studies evaluate different hardware and software products, and by the time the study is completed the technology is often obsolete. In addition, virtually all studies of computers and student learning are based on observational data. Only one randomized experiment that I am aware of has been conducted, and that was done in the late 1970s with a fairly small sample. In addition, computer-based instruction could affect several outcomes to varying degrees, and some studies focus on different outcomes, further clouding conclusions.

The study that utilized random assignment is described in a report by Marjorie Ragosta and her colleagues.[14] The study was conducted by the Educational Testing Service (ETS) with funding from the National Institute of Education. In spring 1977, four elementary schools in the Los Angeles Unified School District were equipped with computer labs using terminals and printers operated by a minicomputer, for 3.5 years beginning in the spring of 1977. Computer-assisted instruction was provided by drill and practice curriculums in math, reading, and language arts. The software was leased from Computer Curriculum Corporation of Palo Alto, California. As part of the research design, students were randomly assigned to receive or not receive CAI curriculum. Students were tested with the Iowa Tests of Basic Skills (ITBS) and the Comprehensive Tests of Basic Skills (CTBS), as well as curriculum-based tests. The results were encouraging. After three years, the average student who received CAI math instruction scored in the 76th percentile of the control group on the CTBS computation test, the 54th percentile on the CTBS concepts test, and the 60th percentile on the CTBS applications test.[15] The average student who received CAI instruction in reading scored better than the average student in the control group, but the gap was only statistically significant in the first of the three and a half years of the experiment.

The ETS experiment was based on a small sample (usually fewer than 200 students in the treatments and controls), and the technology is now dated. It is unclear whether the results apply to students today. But a great advantage of the ETS study is that, in principle, the randomized design ensured that extraneous factors that are correlated with computer use and student achievement (e.g., family income) did not confound the results.

Another study that devoted a good deal of attention to potential spurious factors that might be correlated with the prevalence of computer use and student achievement was conducted by Joshua Angrist and Victor Lavy.[16] Angrist and Lavy exploited variations in the adoption of computers caused by the Tomorrow-98 program, which abruptly and significantly upgraded the computer technology in several schools in Israel. Between 1994 and 1996, the program provided a total of 35,000 computers and teacher instruction to 905 schools. The selection of schools to receive the computer installation was based on an application process that gave priority to towns with a high proportion of seventh and eighth grade enrollment in stand-alone middle schools. Angrist and Lavy concluded: "The results reported here do not support the view that CAI improves learning, at least as measured by pupil test scores. Using a variety of estimation strategies, we find a consistently negative relationship between the program-induced use of computers and fourth-grade math scores."[17] It is unclear, however, whether the bleak results for Israel provide any insight into the possible effect of the use of CAI with American students and with the instructional software packages commonly used in American schools.

As mentioned above, a large-scale study of the impact of computer use on the academic achievement of American students was recently conducted by Harold Wenglinsky.[18] This study received much attention in the press. Wenglinsky modeled students' test scores on the fourth and eighth grade NAEP Mathematics exam as a function of their frequency of computer use in school, type of computer application, class size, students' socioeconomic status, and teachers' characteristics. Although it is hard to determine the exact statistical model that Wenglinsky estimated, it is clear that his findings are mixed. The frequency of school-based computer use was negatively associated with test scores for both fourth and eighth graders. That is, students who reported using a computer more frequently tended to score lower on the NAEP exam. On the other hand, Wenglinsky found that certain computer applications were associated with higher test scores in his estimates. Computer use for applications and simulations was positively associated with test scores, whereas use of computers for drills and practice was negatively associated with test scores. One concern with these results is that they may spuriously reflect a tendency of teachers to use more basic applications when they have weaker students in their class, rather than reflect any direct effect of the technology. No one would be surprised if teachers tended to use traditional drill and practice exercises (e.g., flash cards) with eighth grade students when those students were low-achievers, or if teachers emphasized applications of the integral calculus when their students were high achievers. But one would be reluctant to ascribe causality as running from the teaching method to student achievement in these situations. In a similar fashion, the causality could run from students in need of remedial help to basic drill and practice computer applications, rather than from basic computer applications causing a decline in tests.

Researchers have conducted several meta-analyses on the effect of computer use on student achievement.[19] These studies try to synthesize the underlying estimates in the literature. The meta-analyses tend to find that computer use is positively associated with student achievement. For example, Chen-Lin Kulik and James Kulik surveyed 254 controlled studies of the effectiveness of computer-based instruction (CBI) and concluded that, "In 202 (81 percent) of the studies, the students in the CBI class had the higher examination average; in 46 (19 percent) of the studies, the students in the conventionally taught class had the higher average."[20] Of course, a meta-analysis can only be as convincing as the combined strength of the underlying studies in the literature. If, as in the case of computer use, reverse causality is a problem (e.g., more advantaged students tend to use computers), then a meta-analysis is unlikely to be very informative unless the underlying studies have dealt adequately with the reverse causality problem (which most have not). After reviewing several meta-analyses, single studies, and critical reviews, Larry Cuban and Heather Kirkpatrick conclude, "we are unable to ascertain whether computers in classrooms have in fact been or will be the boon they have promised to be."[21]

My reading of the evidence is that computer-assisted instruction, when done correctly, can probably help reinforce traditional classroom learning. But the curriculum has to be tailored to the student with clear goals in mind, and CAI may be ineffective, or perhaps harmful, if done incorrectly. Discerning cause from effect in the observational studies of computer use and student achievement is nearly an insurmountable challenge for researchers. As I have written elsewhere, the time is past due for the Department of Education to conduct a large-scale, randomized study of the efficacy of computer-assisted instruction to determine which modes of CAI work best and for which types of students. In the meantime, we putter around with highly imperfect information.

THE JOB MARKET AND COMPUTER LITERACY

Workers who use a computer on the job tend to be paid more than other workers in the same industry who have the same level of education and experience but do not use a computer on the job. Moreover, temporary help firms report that, if two workers are otherwise identical but one has computer skills and the other doesn't, they would pay considerably more to the worker with computer skills.[22] In a survey of more than 3,000 employers in Atlanta, Boston, Detroit, and Los Angeles, Harry Holzer asked which types of tasks are performed by newly hired employees. For non-college graduates, he found that 51 percent of newly filled jobs required daily computer use. He also found that a large number of other cognitive tasks were performed in these jobs on a daily basis, including doing arithmetic (65 percent), reading paragraphs (55 percent), and writing paragraphs (30 percent).[23] For college graduates, Holzer found that 74 percent of new hires were required to perform computer tasks on a daily basis.[24] Michael Boozer, Shari Wolkon and I found that students who used computers in high school were more likely to obtain higher paying jobs that involved some computer use early in their career.[25]

In earlier work, I have leaned towards a causal interpretation of the relationship between earnings and computer use. That is, I suspected that if workers who are currently unable to use computers were trained to use them, their wages would increase, on average. In addition, based on Holzer's survey work, I would suspect that workers trained to use computers would also experience less difficulty finding a job (i.e., unemployment would decline).

John DiNardo and Jorn-Steffen Pischke questioned my causal interpretation of the wage premium associated with using a computer on the job. They used data from Germany to estimate earnings functions similar to the ones I estimated for the U.S. First, they showed that the coefficient on a dummy variable indicating computer use at work is similar in magnitude in Germany and the U.S. Next, they showed that a dummy variable measuring such activities as using a pencil at work has an effect on earnings that is similar in magnitude to the computer-use premium when the pencil-use dummy variable is included in the wage equation instead of the computer-use dummy variable. Because they presume pencil use has a spurious effect on earnings, they concluded that one needs to be wary that computer use at work also has a spurious effect.[26]

Their paper serves as a useful reminder that causality cannot be established without an experiment or a well-identified structural model and theory. At the same time, however, one has to be aware that a spurious relationship also cannot be established without an experiment or a well-identified structural model and theory. For example, the effect of computer use on pay may not be spurious even if the effect of pencil use on pay is spurious and similar in magnitude to the computer premium.[27] Equally important, when DiNardo and Pischke controlled for both computer use and pencil use simultaneously in a wage regression using their most recent data, they found that computer use continues to have a substantial impact on pay, but pencil use has a statistically and economically insignificant effect. To the extent that pencil use controls for omitted factors such as inherent cognitive ability, it is computer use that seems to matter for pay and not these other variables. Finally, even if computer use does spuriously pick up the effect of other variables (e.g., inherent ability) in the German labor market, it is not clear that computer training would be of no help in the United States labor market. Nonetheless, DiNardo and Pischke are right to emphasize that a causal interpretation of the effect of computer skills on pay is based on circumstantial evidence and has not been proven beyond a shadow of a doubt.

The role of computer skills in influencing individuals' job prospects and pay is of particular importance to the African American community because, as Table 3.7 shows, black workers are considerably less likely than white workers to use computers on the job. In 1997, 52 percent of white workers directly used a computer on the job, and only 40 percent of black workers did so. The Commerce Department's 1999 report, *Falling Through the Net*, further shows that minorities are much less likely to have access to computers and the Internet at work and at home. If possessing computer skills and having access to information technology are important entry-tickets to high-paying jobs, then fewer black workers can gain entrance.

Table 3.8 reports the types of tasks that workers used computers to perform, by workers' race and Hispanic origin. The sample is restricted to the subset of workers who used a computer on the job. A worker could report multiple tasks, so the sum of the percentages exceeds 100 percent. It is interesting that the general pattern of computer use is similar across racial groups, although black workers reported a lower percentage of use on every task. Even when using a computer on the job, black workers tended to use the computer for fewer tasks than white workers.

CONCLUSION

A great irony of the digital divide is that computers and information technology have tremendous potential to create a color-blind society. Neither the seller nor the buyer of a product over the web knows the race, sex, or ethnicity of the other party involved in the transaction, nor do they care. An Internet search engine designed to seek out the lowest price of a product does not take race, sex, or ethnicity into account. Alas, advanced technology can also exacerbate existing divisions and inequalities in society if minority groups lack the resources, training, and access to the social networks that are required to participate in the digital economy.

What can be done to narrow the digital divide in access to information technology? First, it should be noted that some progress has been made. The decline in the black-white gap in the use of computers in elementary and middle schools — and its elimination in high school — are positive developments. But the more recent opening of a black-white gap in the use of the Internet is a worrisome development. Black students seem to lag behind in using the latest technology in school, and their teachers seem to lag behind in their preparation to use this technology. If the pace of technological change in education hastens, the digital divide in training students will likely widen.

An obvious proposal to try to narrow the digital divide is to invest more to expand training and access to information technology. As then Commerce Secretary William Daley has argued, "Ensuring access to the fundamental tools of the digital economy is one of the most significant investments our nation can make."[28] To some extent, such an investment is already taking place, but so far it has not been adequate to bridge the gap in school resources, teacher preparation, and home resources, and to keep up with the rapid pace of technological change. It also seems to me that there is a need to develop and distribute instructional materials that are geared to the minority community. For example, as an outgrowth of his senior thesis at the University of California, Berkeley, in 1992 Eno Essien wrote and self-published an excellent and widely used manual titled *The Black Computer Survival Guide*, which illustrated the use of key computer software with examples specifically developed for the minority community. More current manuals of this sort could help spread interest in, and encourage the use of, information technology in minority communities.

Most workers learned how to use a computer on the job because the technology was in a nascent stage when they were in school. One issue to consider is the role of social networks in allocating workers to jobs and therefore to on-the-job training. Even for non-college jobs, Holzer found that social networks were an important aspect of job placement: 26 percent of newly hired non-college employees were recruited for their job via a referral by a current employee.[29] Minority workers are underrepresented in positions that use computers, and this may be a barrier to gaining entry to jobs and networks where workers are trained to use computers. If this is the case, then encouraging firms to cast a broader net in recruiting could expand access to information technology. In addition, temporary help firms are a major source of training on computers and often provide a path to a permanent job.[30] Alerting individuals of training opportunities, such as those provided by temporary help firms, could also help expand access to information technology.

Finally, nearly two million Americans are currently in jail or prison. This population is more than 90 percent male, and minorities are overrepresented. Only a very small proportion of individuals who are incarcerated work while they are in prison. And a distressingly low proportion of individuals who have been incarcerated work in the formal economy after they have been released. It might be possible to reach out to those who are incarcerated to try to prepare them for a meaningful career when they are released. Indeed, there have been some exemplary cases in which prisoners were introduced to information technology in a meaningful way. For example, the Detwiler Foundation has worked with prisons to train prison laborers to refurbish obsolete computers that were donated by corporations. The prisoners upgrade the computers, which are then donated to schools — a win-win situation. Successfully bridging the digital divide may require similar creative solutions.

* * *

The author, who wrote this paper while on leave at the Center for Advanced Study in the Behavioral Sciences at Stanford University, is grateful to Melissa Rekas for her excellent research assistance.

TABLE 3.1

PERCENT OF STUDENTS USING A COMPUTER IN SCHOOL, BY RACE AND HISPANIC ORIGIN

	1984	1989	1993	1997
All Grades				
All Races	31.3	51.2	66.3	77.0
White	33.7	53.6	68.4	78.4
Black	17.9	39.3	56.5	72.1
Asian	n/a	46.8	62.4	71.1
American Indian	n/a	56.5	69.8	74.1
Hispanic	20.2	41.5	58.1	67.7
Grades 1-8				
All Races	32.7	54.4	69.2	79.6
White	35.7	57.8	71.9	81.5
Black	16.7	38.2	56.9	72.
Asian	n/a	48.0	63.3	74.3
American Indian	n/a	57.8	71.8	79.2
Hispanic	19.6	42.1	59.1	68.8
Grades 9-12				
All Races	28.5	43.4	59.2	71.5
White	29.8	43.6	59.8	71.8
Black	20.5	42.2	55.5	72.6
Asian	n/a	43.7	59.9	64.7
American Indian	n/a	52.5	62.8	64.8
Hispanic	21.7	39.5	55.6	65.1

Sample includes all children aged 6-18 in grades 1-12, and excludes students classified as "other" race, and excludes students with a missing value for computer use in school. Hispanics may be of any race.

Source: Author's calculations from the October CPS. The CPS final weights were used to calculate the percentages. See Appendix Tables 3a and 3b for standard errors and sample sizes.

TABLE 3.2

PERCENT OF STUDENTS USING THE INTERNET
IN SCHOOL, OCTOBER 1997

	Percent	Standard Error	Sample Size
All Grades			
All Races	19.45%	0.30	22,435
White	20.52	0.30	18,109
Black	14.81	0.60	3,023
Asian	16.84	1.30	868
American Indian	21.66	1.97	435
Hispanic	11.76	0.60	2,639
Grades 1-8			
All Races	16.49	0.30	15,332
White	17.27	0.30	12,352
Black	12.79	0.70	2,089
Asian	15.21	1.47	591
American Indian	20.31	2.30	300
Hispanic	9.99	0.70	1,880
Grades 9-12			
All Races	25.69	0.50	7,103
White	27.38	0.60	5,757
Black	19.13	1.30	934
Asian	20.20	2.40	277
American Indian	24.12	3.70	135
Hispanic	15.85	1.30	759

Sample includes all children aged 6-18 in grades 1-12 and excludes all classified as ""other" race. Hispanics may be of any race. Percentages were calculated as weighted averages, using the "CPS final weight as weights.

Source: Author's calculations from October 1997 CPS.

TABLE 3.3

LINEAR PROBABILITY MODEL FOR COMPUTER USE, 1984

Dependent variable: One if uses computer in school, zero if not

	1	2	3	4
Intercept	0.352	0.493	0.444	0.490
	(0.003)	(0.026)	(0.030)	(0.034)
Black	-0.172	-0.165	-0.121	-0.088
(1=yes)	(0.008)	(0.008)	(0.009)	(0.009)
Hispanic	-0.147	-0.139	-0.116	-0.087
(1=yes)	(0.011)	(0.011)	(0.011)	(0.011)
Female		-0.022	-0.022	-0.020
(1=yes)		(0.006)	(0.006)	(0.006)
Public school		-0.041	-0.043	-0.025
(1=yes)		(0.010)	(0.010)	(0.010)
Grade		0.028	0.022	0.013
		(0.005)	(0.005)	(0.005)
Age		-0.024	-0.018	-0.011
		(0.004)	(0.004)	(0.004)
Northeast			-0.004	0.001
(1=yes)			(0.010)	(0.010)
Midwest			0.028	0.036
(1=yes)			(0.009)	(0.009)
South			-0.095	-0.091
(1=yes)			(0.009)	(0.009)
3 SMSA type dummies included	no	no	yes	yes
2 SMSA size dummies included	no	no	yes	yes
14 income category dummies included	no	no	no	yes

Notes: Sample size is 25,046. Standard errors are shown in parentheses. Omitted race group is white. Hispanics may be of any race. Sample restricted to children age 6-18, in grades 1-12. Sample excludes individuals with missing values for computer use in school or classified as "other race". SMSA type includes central city, balance of SMSA, non-SMSA and not identifiable (omitted category). SMSA size categories are: not identifiable, 1-3 million, greater than 3 million (omitted category). Income categories are: less than $5,000, 5,000-7,499, 7,500-9,999, 10,000-12,499, 12,500-14,999, 15,000-17,499, 17,500-19,999, 20,000-24,999, 25,000-29,999, 30,000-34,999, 35,000-39,999, 40,000-49,999, 50,000-74,999, 75,000 or higher (omitted category), and income not reported.

TABLE 3.4
LINEAR PROBABILITY MODEL FOR COMPUTER USE, 1989

Dependent variable: One if uses computer in school, zero if not

	1	2	3	4
Intercept	0.553	0.790	0.832	0.740
	(0.004)	(0.028)	(0.033)	(0.036)
Black	-0.157	-0.153	-0.114	-0.085
(1=yes)	(0.009)	(0.009)	(0.010)	(0.010)
Asian	-0.084	-0.088	-0.058	-0.050
(1=yes)	(0.019	(0.019)	(0.020)	(0.020)
American Indian	0.017	0.024	0.031	0.058
(1=yes)	(0.032)	(0.032)	(0.032)	(0.032)
Hispanic	-0.134	-0.132	-0.095	-0.068
(1=yes)	(0.010)	(0.010)	(0.011)	(0.011)
Female		-0.007	-0.007	-0.006
(1=yes)		(0.006)	(0.006)	(0.006)
Public school		-0.020	-0.023	-0.011
(1=yes)		(0.011)	(0.011)	(0.011)
Grade		0.026	0.025	0.018
		(0.005)	(0.005)	(0.005)
Age		-0.033	-0.032	-0.026
		(0.005)	(0.005)	(0.005)
Northeast			0.047	0.049
(1=yes)			(0.011)	(0.011)
Midwest			0.033	0.036
(1=yes)			(0.010)	(0.010)
South			-0.040	-0.036
(1=yes)			(0.010)	(0.010)
3 MSA type dummies included	no	no	yes	yes
7 MSA size dummies included	no	no	yes	yes
14 income category dummies included	no	no	no	yes

Notes: Sample size is 24,291. Standard errors are shown in parentheses. Omitted race group is white. Hispanics may be of any race. Sample restricted to children age 6-18, in grades 1-12. Sample excludes individuals with missing values for computer use in school or classified as "other race". SMSA type includes central city of MSA, not in center city but in MSA, not in MSA, and not identified (omitted category). SMSA size categories are: not identified, 100,000-249,999, 250,000-499,999, 500,000-999,999, 1-2.499 million (omitted), 2.5-4.999 million, 5-9.999 million, and greater than 10 million. Income categories are: less than $5,000, 5,000-7,499, 7,500-9,999, 10,000-12,499, 12,500-14,999, 15,000-19,999, 20,000-24,999, 25,000-29,999, 30,000-34,999, 35,000-39,999, 40,000-49,999, 50,000-59,999 60,000-74,000, and 75,000 or higher (omitted category), and income not reported.

TABLE 3.5
LINEAR PROBABILITY MODEL FOR COMPUTER USE, 1993

Dependent variable: One if uses computer in school, zero if not

	1	2	3	4
Intercept	0.699	0.880	0.777	0.676
	(0.004)	(0.026)	(0.030)	(0.033)
Black	-0.132	-0.129	-0.102	-0.077
(1=yes)	(0.008)	(0.008)	(0.009)	(0.010)
Asian	-0.074	-0.077	-0.038	-0.036
(1=yes)	(0.018)	(0.018)	(0.018)	(0.018)
American Indian	0.004	0.001	0.010	0.027
(1=yes)	(0.035)	(0.035)	(0.035)	(0.035)
Hispanic	-0.115	-0.114	-0.063	-0.040
(1=yes)	(0.010)	(0.010)	(0.011)	(0.011)
Female		-0.001	-0.002	-0.001
(1=yes)		(0.006)	(0.006)	(0.006)
Public school		-0.024	-0.029	-0.013
(1=yes)		(0.011)	(0.011)	(0.011)
Grade		0.012	0.015	0.009
		(0.005)	(0.005)	(0.005)
Age		-0.020	-0.023	-0.018
		(0.004)	(0.005)	(0.005)
Northeast			0.042	0.043
(1=yes)			(0.010)	(0.010)
Midwest			0.035	0.037
(1=yes)			(0.010)	(0.010)
South			0.005	0.008
(1=yes)			(0.009)	(0.009)
3 MSA type dummies included	no	no	yes	yes
7 MSA size dummies included	no	no	yes	yes
14 income category dummies included	no	no	no	yes

Notes: Sample size is 23,521. Standard errors are shown in parentheses. Omitted race group is white. Hispanics may be of any race. Sample restricted to children age 6-18, grades 1-12. Sample excludes individuals with missing values for computer use in school or classified as "other race". SMSA type includes central city of MSA, not in center in MSA, not in MSA, and not identified (omitted category). SMSA size categories are: not identified, 100,000-249,999, 250,000-499,999, 500,000-999,999, 1-2.499 million (omitted), 2.5-4.999 million, 5-9.999 million, and greater than 10 million. Income categories are: less than $5,000, 5,000-7,499, 7,500-9,999, 10,000-12,499, 12,500-14,999, 15,000-19,999, 20,000-24,999, 25,000-29,999, 30,000-34,999, 35,000-39,999, 40,000-49,999, 50,000-59,999, 60,000-74,000, and 75,000 or higher (omitted category), and income not reported.

TABLE 3.6
LINEAR PROBABILITY MODEL FOR COMPUTER USE, 1997

Dependent variable: One if uses computer in school, zero if not

	1	2	3	4
Intercept	0.805	0.968	0.872	0.822
	(0.003)	(0.024)	(0.029)	(0.031)
Black (1=yes)	-0.081	-0.080	-0.064	-0.045
	(0.008)	(0.008)	(0.008)	(0.009)
Asian (1=yes)	-0.092	-0.093	-0.048	-0.046
	(0.014)	(0.014)	(0.015)	(0.015)
American Indian (1=yes)	-0.044	-0.039	-0.035	-0.023
	(0.024)	(0.024)	(0.024)	(0.024)
Hispanic (1=yes)	-0.125	-0.127	-0.084	-0.064
	(0.008)	(0.008)	(0.009)	(0.009)
Female (1=yes)		-0.012	-0.013	-0.012
		(0.006)	(0.006)	(0.006)
Public school (1=yes)		-0.004	-0.014	-0.004
		(0.010)	(0.010)	(0.010)
Grade		0.015	0.020	0.017
		(0.004)	(0.004)	(0.004)
Age		-0.021	-0.026	-0.024
		(0.004)	(0.004)	(0.004)
Northeast (1=yes)			0.039	0.040
			(0.009)	(0.009)
Midwest (1=yes)			0.067	0.067
			(0.009)	(0.009)
South (1=yes)			0.042	0.044
			(0.008)	(0.008)
3 MSA type dummies included	no	no	yes	yes
6 MSA size dummies included	no	no	yes	yes
14 income category dummies included	no	no	no	yes

Notes: Sample size is 22,435. Standard errors are shown in parentheses. Omitted race group is white. Hispanics may be of any race. Sample restricted to children age 6-18, in grades 1-12. Sample excludes individuals with missing values for computer use in school "or classified as "other race". SMSA type includes central city of MSA, not in center city but in MSA, not in MSA, and not identified (omitted category). SMSA size categories are: not identified, 100,000-249,999, 250,000-499,999, 500,000-999,999, 1-2.499 million (omitted), 2.5-4.999 million, and greater than 5 million. Income categories are: less than $5,000, 5,000-7,499, 7,500-9,999, 10,000-12,499, 12,500-14,999, 15,000-19,999, 20,000-24,999, 25,000-29,999, 30,000-34,999, 35,000-39,999, 40,000-49,999, 50,000-59,999, 60,000-74,000, and 75,000 or higher (omitted category), and income not reported.

TABLE 3.7
PERCENT OF WORKERS WHO USE A COMPUTER AT WORK 1997

	Percent	Standard Error	Sample Size
All Races	50.63	0.2	56,247
White	52.06	0.2	48,553
Black	40.47	0.7	4,930
Asian	51.46	1.1	2,128
American Indian	37.02	1.9	636
Hispanic	30.33	0.7	4,675

Sample includes employed persons aged 18 to 64 and excludes those classified as "other" race. Hispanics may be of any race

TABLE 3.8
USES OF COMPUTERS AT WORK IN1997, BY RACE AND HISPANIC ORIGIN

Percent of workers who use a computer for various tasks

	All Races	White	Black	Asian	American Indian	Hispanic
Word Processing	57.1	57.5	51.9	60.4	51.4	49.9
Calendar/ Scheduling	.37.7	38.0	36.0	35.1	41.8	33.8
Email/ Communications	47.1	47.4	43.5	50.7	39.8	40.6
Bookkeeping	30.2	31.0	24.3	24.7	26.2	24.4
Customer records & accounts	50.8	51.6	46.7	42.7	49.6	49.4
Inventory Control	28.8	29.2	27.7	22.1	30.1	31.9
Invoicing	24.1	24.7	19.6	20.3	24.5	23.3
Sales & Marketing	22.1	22.9	17.3	15.3	19.8	18.9
Desktop Publishing	15.3	15.8	12.4	10.7	20.7	10.9
Graphics & Design	20.5	21.0	16.3	18.8	24.8	16.2
Analysis	26.9	27.4	20.8	31.8	23.9	21.3
Programming	15.1	15.0	14.0	20.4	13.0	10.5
Spreadsheets	32.6	33.2	26.2	34.4	25.2	24.4
Databases	34.2	34.5	29.4	37.7	36.4	27.1
Other	12.6	12.7	12.5	10.8	12.2	12.1
Sample Size	28,762	25,433	2,016	1,076	237	1,407

Notes: Sample includes employed persons aged 18 to 64 and excludes those classified as "other" race. Sample includes only persons who report directly using a computer at work. Hispanics may be of any race. The sum of the percentages exceed 100 because individuals could report multiple tasks.

APPENDIX TABLE 3A
STANDARD ERRORS FOR TABLE 3.1

All Grades	1984	1989	1993	1997
All Races	0.30%	0.30%	0.30%	0.30%
White	0.30%	0.40%	0.30%	0.30%
Black	0.60%	0.80%	0.90%	0.80%
Asian	n/a	1.90%	1.60%	1.50%
American Indian	n/a	2.70%	2.20%	2.10%
Hispanic	0.90%	1.10%	1.00%	0.90%
Grades 1-8				
All Races	0.40%	0.40%	0.40%	0.30%
White	0.40%	0.40%	0.40%	0.30%
Black	0.80%	1.00%	1.00%	1.00%
Asian	n/a	2.30%	1.90%	1.80%
American Indian	n/a	3.00%	2.50%	2.30%
Hispanic	1.10%	1.30%	1.20%	1.10%
Grades 9-12				
All Races	0.50%	0.60%	0.60%	0.50%
White	0.50%	0.60%	0.70%	0.60%
Black	1.20%	1.60%	1.70%	1.50%
Asian	n/a	3.60%	3.20%	2.90%
American Indian	n/a	5.70%	5.10%	4.10%
Hispanic	18.00%	2.20%	2.00%	1.70%

APPENDIX TABLE 3B
SAMPLE SIZES FOR TABLE 3.1

	1984	1989	1993	1997
All Grades				
All Races	25,046	24,291	23,521	22,435
White	21,568	19,931	19,090	18,109
Black	3,478	3,331	3,141	3,023
Asian	0	682	871	868
American Indian	0	347	419	435
Hispanic	1,895	1,964	2,214	2,639
Grades 1-8				
All Races	16,936	17,271	16,728	15,332
White	14,504	14,106	13,520	12,352
Black	2,432	2,404	2,241	2,089
Asian	0	492	640	591
American Indian	0	269	327	300
Hispanic	1,387	1,466	1,599	1,880
Grades 9-12				
All Races	8,110	7,020	6,793	7,103
White	7,064	5,825	5,570	5,757
Black	1,046	927	900	934
Asian	0	190	231	277
American Indian	0	78	92	135
Hispanic	508	498	615	759

NOTES

1. See Alan Krueger, "How Computers Have Changed the Wage Structure: Evidence from Microdata, 1984-1989," *Quarterly Journal of Economics* 108, no. 1 (February 1993): 33-61; Harry Holzer, *What Employers Want* (New York: Russell Sage Foundation, 1996); and David Autor, Lawrence Katz, and Alan Krueger, "*Computing Inequality: Have Computers Changed the Labor Market?*" Quarterly Journal of Economics 113, no. 4 (November 1998): 1169-1213.

2. U.S. Department of Commerce, National Telecommunications and Information Administration, *Falling Through the Net: Defining the Digital Divide* (Washington, DC: 1999).

3. One prominent study, which did not find a racial gap in computer use in school, was done by the University of Minnesota for the National Science Foundation. It was based on the 1981-82 National Assessment of Science, which included a national random sample of 18,000 students aged 9, 13, and 17 (see Irving McPhail, "Computer Inequities in School Uses of Microcomputers: Policy Implications," *Journal of Negro Education* 54, no. 1 (1985): 3-13.

4. Henry Becker, "How Schools Use Microcomputers: Summary of the 1983 National Survey" (Second National Survey of Instructional Uses of School Computers, Johns Hopkins University, Baltimore, MD, 1985).

5. Henry Becker and Carleton Sterling, "Equity in School Computer Use: National Data and Neglected Considerations," *Journal of Educational Computing* Research 3, no. 3 (1987): 289-311.

6. Ronald Anderson, Vicki Lundmark, Linda Harris, Shon Magnan, "Equity in Computing," in *Social Issues in Computing*, ed. Chuck Huff and Thomas Finholt (New York: McGraw-Hill, 1994).

7. Michael Boozer, Alan Krueger, and Shari Wolkon, "Race and School Quality Since Brown vs. Board of Education," in *Brookings Papers on Economic Activity: Microeconomics*, ed. Martin N. Baily and Clifford Winston (Washington, DC: Brookings Institution, 1992): 269-326.

8. Harold Wenglinsky, "Does It Compute? The Relationship Between Educational Technology and Student Achievement in Mathematics" (Unpublished paper for the Policy Information Center, Research Division, Educational Testing Service, Princeton, NJ, 1998).

9. Wenglinsky, "Does It Compute?"

10. Respondents were told that for purposes of the survey, computer use excluded "hand-held calculators or games, electronic video games, notepads, WebTV, or systems which do not use a typewriter-like keyboard."

11. Logit models yielded results that were quite similar to the linear probability models, so the linear probability models were reported for simplicity. Because all of the explanatory variables in the model are dummy variables, it is not surprising that the logits and the linear probability models are similar.

12. The coefficient on the black indicator variable is not equal to the difference between the proportions using a computer in Table 1 because Hispanic students can be of any race, so the variables are not mutually orthogonal.

13. These figures are for students ages 6 to 14 in 1997.

14. Marjorie Ragosta, Paul Holland, and Dean Jamison, "Computer-Assisted Instruction and Compensatory Education: The ETS/LAUSD Study" (Final Report, ETS,

Princeton, NJ, April 1982).

15. The treatment-control difference was only statistically significant on the computation test, however.

16. Joshua Angrist and Victor Lavy, "New Evidence on Classroom Computers and Pupil Learning" (Massachusetts Institute of Technology, Cambridge, MA, May 1999, mimeographed).

17. Angrist and Lavy, "New Evidence on Classroom Computers."

18. Wenglinsky, "Does It Compute?"

19. See Larry Cuban and Heather Kirkpatrick, "Computers Make Kids Smarter—Right?" *Technos* 7, no. 2 (Summer 1998): 62-31, for a summary of the meta-analyses on this topic and several individual studies.

20. Chen-Lin Kulik and James Kulik, "Effectiveness of Computer-Based Instruction: An Updated Analysis," *Computers in Human Behavior* 7 (1991): 75-94.

21. Cuban and Kirkpatrick, "Computers Make Kids Smarter."

22. Krueger, "How Computers Have Changed the Wage Structure."

23. Holzer, *What Employers Want.*

24. Harry Holzer, "Employer Skill Needs and Labor Market Outcomes" (Michigan State University, East Lansing, MI, September 1995, mimeographed).

25. Boozer, Krueger, and Wolkon, "Race and School Quality."

26. John DiNardo and Jorn-Steffen Pischke, "The Returns to Computer Use Revisited: Have Pencils Changed the Wage Structure Too?" *Quarterly Journal of Economics* (February 1997).

27. Or put another way, if pencils have a spurious effect on pay, why not conclude that education, experience, and all the other variables in the wage equation also have a spurious effect?

28. Department of Commerce, *Falling Through the Net.*

29. Holzer, *What Employers Want.*

30. David H. Autor, "Why Do Temporary Help Firms Provide Free General Skills Training?" (chapter from unpublished Ph.D. dissertation, Harvard University, 1999).

Chapter Four

RACIAL AND ETHNIC DIFFERENCES IN THE IMPACT OF JOB TRAINING ON WAGES

William M. Rodgers III

Researchers and policy makers continue to be concerned with the existence of the sizeable and persistent black-white wage gap[1]. A critical issue for public policy is whether this wage gap can be reduced through traditional job training programs and equal employment opportunity policies or whether other strategies are required. If, as some scholars argue, the black-white wage gap reflects racial differences in the acquisition of pre-labor market skills, then the effectiveness of on-the-job training programs and of equal employment opportunity policies is limited. On the other hand, if the racial wage gap reflects racial differences in skills acquired in the labor market or labor market discrimination, then an effective public policy must address these disparities.

Several recent studies support the first position — that pre-market factors explain the black-white wage gap. Several researchers[2] have found that differences in the composite score on the Armed Forces Qualifications Test (AFQT), a purported measure of pre-labor market skills and abilities, explain most if not all of the black-white wage gap. However, my research (with William Spriggs) challenges this conclusion.[3] We presented evidence that the composite AFQT score is a racially biased predictor of wages. When we removed the bias, the black-white wage gap remained large. Arthur Goldsmith and colleagues obtained a large black-white wage gap after controlling for AFQT scores and a set of psychological constructs like self esteem and locus of control. Using a score from a sentence completion exam as a measure of skill, Patrick Mason

William Rodgers is the Frances L. and Edwin L. Cummings Associate Professor of Economics at the College of William and Mary and director of the college's Center for the Study of Equality.

also obtained a large black-white wage gap.[4] Most recently (in 2002), William Spriggs and I provided an objective comparison of estimates of the black-white wage gap found earlier by N. Maxwell (1994) and by me and Spriggs (1996).[5] They show that the size of the gap depends solely on how each study treats the AFQT score. If a large wage gap remains after controlling for differences in human capital and in pre-labor market skill, it suggests that either there are racial differences in productive skills acquired during adulthood or labor market discrimination.

This paper investigates racial differences in the productive skill acquired during adulthood — specifically, the skills acquired through formal, on-the-job training. First, I explore racial differences in the receipt and content of training. Then, I estimate the impact of racial differences in formal job training on black-white wage differences.

Past studies have found a link between racial differences in the receipt of job training and the black-white wage gap. Greg Duncan and Saul Hoffman analyzed a 1975 Panel Study of Income Dynamics sample of working household heads and wives. They found that black men had lower participation rates than white males, and that this difference accounted for almost one-fifth of the male wage gap.[6] Mary Corcoran and Greg Duncan analyzed a sample similar to that just cited, but examined only individuals who worked at least 500 hours. Using an Oaxaca-Blinder decomposition of the black-white wage gap, they found that the number of years of on-the-job training explained 15 percent of the male black-white wage gap, and 8 percent of the wage gap between white males and black females.[7] Finally, Edwin Sexton and Reed Olsen found that in 1975, training was less portable for blacks than whites.[8] Further, the training gap between whites and blacks did not narrow from 1975 to 1985, nor did the training that blacks receive become more portable.

Although these findings suggest that racial differences in skills acquired as adults in the labor market contribute to the black-white wage gap, there are some problems. First, these studies describe the role that racial differences in training prior to 1985 play in explaining black -white wage gaps among prime-age workers. Given that the wage gap's recent expansion occurred among the cohort that entered the labor market during the 1980s, this evidence is not the most up-to-date. Second, the training information used in these early studies was not very detailed. Identifying racial differences in the type of training received is potentially important because the economic returns to training vary by type.[9] Finally, although the older studies included controls for racial differences in years of formal schooling, they did not account for racial differences in other pre-market factors — such as school quality, family culture, and parental investments in children — that might lead to differences in labor quality. The link between racial differences in job training and the black-white wage gap might be less strong if these factors were included in the analysis.

This paper addresses all of these concerns. To do this, I use the National Longitudinal Survey of Youth (NLSY), the most complete and comprehensive data set available on cognitive skills, work experience, and training. The NLSY data is more recent than that used in earlier studies of on the job training and it contains more detailed information about the type and content of formal training. In addition, the longitudinal structure of the NLSY provides an opportunity to assess the contribution of pre-market factors to the black-white wage gap without relying on a racially biased test score.

The findings reconfirm the importance of racial differences in post labor market experiences. Training gaps in the types of training that yield the greatest economic rewards exist; however, these differences explain very little of the black-white wage gap. Informal training as measured by actual experience and tenure at current job explains a larger portion of the black-white wage gap than participation in formal training programs. Even after accounting for differences in pre-market factors, experience and job training, I estimate a black-white wage gaps of 4.8 percent among women and 9.6 percent among men, instead of 2.3 percent among women and a 7 percent gap among men in regression models that include the AFQT as a predictor variable.

DATA

The NLSY is a longitudinal data set of 10,000 young adults who have been interviewed annually since 1979.[10] At the survey's beginning, the youth were 14 to 22 years of age. Since the 1988 interview, detailed information has been collected on participation in firm-provided job training programs. At each interview, respondents were asked to describe whether they received any type of training since the last interview.[11] If the respondents answered "yes", then they were asked to describe whether the program was an on-the-job such as an apprenticeship or or company program, or an off-the-job program such as a business school, a vocational technical or trade school or a correspondence course. Respondents also describe the length of the training programs.

Apprenticeship programs are formal programs in which an individual agrees to work in return for wages and training in a skilled trade or art for a predetermined amount of time. Business programs refer to classes that are not taken for college credit at either the undergraduate or graduate level. Vocational programs include any vocational or technical school program such as beauty, auto mechanic, and welder schools. Correspondence training refers to programs offered through the mail. Seminar training covers a wide variety of programs. They range from the provision of new information on the latest developments in one's field (e.g., changes in accounting law, advances in computer technology, or new medical techniques) to the development of general skills such as management, leadership or public speaking. Attendance at professional meetings, seminars on personal finance, and lifestyle improvements are also examples.

The samples are based on the following restrictions. Respondents are required to have completed their formal schooling as of the 1988 interview date, and had wage observations and information on other variables in the 1988 to 1994 interviews. Our final sample is a group of 478 African American women, 1,102 white women, 572 African American men, and 1,331 white men. We observe them in each year from 1988 to 1994. Pooling the observations across time lead to 1,680 African American female-year observations, 3,651 white female-year observations, 1,992 African American male-year observations, and 4,487 white male-year observations. The panel is unbalanced because respondents might have been unemployed or out of the labor force at the time of an interview.

THE INCIDENCE OF TRAINING

Table 4.1 provides information on the receipt of training in our sample. Panels A and B are for women and men, respectively. The participation rates indicate that company programs are the most common for men and women of both races, yet modest racial differences exist. The participation rates of white and African American women are similar. The participation rate of white men is 1.8 percentage points higher than the rate of African American men. The largest racial gap in training participation is in seminars outside work. Between 3 and 4.5 percent of white men and women reported participating in seminars outside of work, compared to 0.9 to 1.5 for African American men and women. African American women have higher participation rates in vocational programs.

To identify the factors that might explain the racial training gaps shown in

Table 4.1, I use a probit model to predict participation in company, apprentice-ship, vocational and seminar programs as a function of worker and firm charac-teristics. The estimated coefficients and their partial derivatives are reported in Appendix Table 4A. Table 4.2 summarizes the effects of worker and firm char-acteristics on the probability of receipt of training, by type of training and by sex of worker.

Consistent with earlier studies of participation rates, employees of large firms are more likely to participate in in-house company training programs. Education increases the probability of participation in both company and out-side seminar training, but decreases the probability of receipt of vocational training for men. The effects of experience, union membership, sector of employment, local labor market conditions and geography vary by type of train-ing and sex of worker.

The racial gap in company-provided training disappears for both men and women once we control for differences in education, work experience, marital status, geography, firm size, and industry. Race is not a statistically significant determinant of the receipt of company training for either women or men. On average, black women have 0.11 years less schooling than white women, and this differential tends to widen the gap in participation in company training. However, the impact of schooling is offset by African American women's employment in larger firms and their residence in areas with slightly lower unemployment rates. As a result, black and white women have similar rates of participation in company, in-house training.

For men, the gap in receipt of company training is explained by racial dif-ferences in years of schooling and in years of experience. The mean years of schooling for black men in the sample is 12.32 and for white men 12.69, a dif-ference of 0.37 years. The average work experience of black male workers is 57 weeks less than that of white male workers. Again, the concentration of African Americans in larger firms tends to increase the probability that they receive company training, narrowing the black-white gap in participation.

Controlling for worker and employer characteristics does not eliminate the racial difference in seminar participation. Racial differences in years of schooling explain some, but not all, of the lower participation of African Americans in seminars. Other contributing factors for men include their lower marriage rates and their geographic distribution (outside of the Midwest and not in suburbs). The concentration of African American women in larger firms tends to lower their participation rates, but their job tenure and their residence in areas with lower unemployment rates tends to increase their participation rates. Black women and men have a lower probability of receivingseminar training, other factors held constant.

There are several plausible explanations for this racial gap in participation. One, the gap in training reflects differences in the distribution of black and white workers within the broad industry categories described in Table 4.1. For example, "Business and Repair Services" encompasses activities ranging from "Computer Programming Services" to " Handbill Distribution Services." The need for skill improvement is likely to vary dramatically across these employers. Furthermore, within industries, firms with greater commitments to reduction in worker turnover are more likely to offer training. Seminars, by definition, are located off site. Transportation might also be a constraint. Greater reliance of public transportation and longer commutes for African American workers might limit their access to training programs. Finally, blacks may lack information about training opportunities.

It is tempting to attribute the seminar participation gap to greater financial constraints faced by African American workers. Seminar training includes professional seminars on the latest developments in one's field as well as development of general skills like leadership or public speaking. These skills are not likely to be firm specific and hence, workers might be expected to shoulder a larger portion of the cost of seminars than of the cost of company training. However, the same argument applies to vocational training programs and African American women have a higher probability of participation in these programs than do white women, holding other factors constant.

THE BLACK-WHITE WAGE GAP AND THE PAYOFF TO JOB TRAINING

Do differences in the receipt of job training contribute to the black-white wage gaps? To answer this question, several different statistical techniques were utilized. The results are summarized in the different columns of Tables 4.3 and 4.4. Though the size of estimates vary, the results from the different estimations are consistent.

I start with an ordinary least squares (OLS) model of the determinants of wages. The model includes the job training incidence measures in Table 4.1, years of schooling, tenure at current job, and, in addition, information on firm size, industry, public sector employment, region of residence, marital status, metropolitan residence, union membership, and local area unemployment rate. To assess the contribution of pre-market factors, I initially include the AFQT score. However, as discussed above, the AFQT score is a racially biased predictor of wages. Its inclusion in the model is likely to cause an underestimate of the impact of differences in market factors, like receipt of training, that are highly correlated with race.

In a more recent study, Beth Wilson and James Ziliak used an alternative method to assess the contribution of pre-market factors to the black-white wage gap.[12] Instead of controlling directly for pre-market factors with a test score, they controlled for racial differences in pre-labor market factors by estimating correlated random effects models. Their estimation procedure is controversial. To distinguish between race and the time-invariant pre-market factors, a plausible set of instrumental variables is needed.

I utilize the longitudinal structure of the NLSY and a correlated random effects estimator proposed by Hausman and Taylor and used in Ziliak and Wilson and to provide an alternative estimate of the contribution of pre-market factors to the black-white wage gap. I also use the longitudinal structure of the NLSY and the econometric technique to remove the bias that may exist in the estimates of the returns to training.

The wage equation for the ith individual in year t can be written as:

$$lnW_{it} = \alpha_1 X_{it} + \alpha_2 Z_i + \alpha_3 R_i + \alpha_i + \varepsilon_{it}, (1)$$

where lnW_{it} denotes the *ith* individual's log hourly wage in year *t*, X_{it} denotes the *ith* individual's characteristics in year t (e.g., experience and training information), and Z_i denotes the *ith* individual's time invariant AFQT score and years of schooling, a_i denotes a time-invariant person-specific effect which captures the impact that pre-market factors have on wages. In a fixed effect model, the individual coefficients on years of schooling, race and the fixed effects are not identifiable because all time-invariant effects are purged from the model. In order to identify all of the parameters, a random effects model must be estimated. The time-invariant person specific effect is assumed to be random.

Tables 4.3 and 4.4 summarize the findings. Table 4.3 reports the percentage change in earnings associated with a one-unit change in schooling, work experience, job tenure and the age-adjusted AFQT score. Table 4.4 reports the percentage change in earnings associated with receipt of firm-provided training, by type of training. The coefficient estimates for each model specification are reported in Appendix Table 4B.

As described above, I start with OLS models that include the AFQT score. I then exclude the score. Excluding the AFQT score raises the training, years of schooling and experience coefficients, suggesting that the AFQT is correlated with human capital measures. However, the relation does not appear to be that large because the increases in the estimated returns are small. I then estimate random effects and correlated random effects models. Regardless of specification, the results are consistent with past studies of training in the NLSY. Years of schooling, actual experience, tenure at current job and the AFQT score have positive impacts on the wages of whites and African Americans. Company provided training has a positive and significant effect on earnings in almost every model specification for men and women of both races. Receipt of seminar training has a positive effect on earnings of men but it is not always statistically significant. Vocational training and apprenticeships appear to be negatively correlated with earnings, but the estimates are not statistically significant.

Decompositions in the next section will demonstrate that the differences in the receipt of company and seminar training contribute to the racial wage gap because company and seminars are the most financially lucrative. However, compared to racial differences in years of schooling, actual work experience, tenure at current job and cognitive skills, the contribution will be small. The returns to training appear to be similar for African Americans and whites, thus contributing little to the gap, while racial differences in returns to schooling and actual experience will exacerbate the size of the wage gap. African Americans have less experience and tenure, but they also receive smaller economic returns for the same experience.

DECOMPOSING THE BLACK-WHITE WAGE GAP

Several models have been proposed in the literature to estimate labor market discrimination. Using a version of Equation (1) that excludes the fixed effect, the first decomposition can be written as:

$$\overline{\ln W_w} - \overline{\ln W_b} = (\overline{X_w} - \overline{X_b})\, \alpha + \alpha_3$$

where the left-hand term denotes the average wage gap between whites and African Americans. It can be decomposed into two portions. The first is the predicted wage gap due to differences in the average characteristics of whites and African Americans. The coefficients are based on a regression that pools the data about these two racial groups. The second term, α_3 denotes the unexplained wage gap or difference in the intercepts of whites and African Americans. This portion is commonly referred to as discrimination. It measures the unexplained wage gap between observationally equivalent whites and African Americans.

The second decomposition models discrimination as racial differences in the economic returns. It can be written as:

$$\overline{\ln W_w} - \overline{\ln W_b} = (\,\overline{X_w} - \overline{X_b}\,)\ \alpha + X_w\,(\alpha_w + \alpha) + X_b(\alpha + \alpha_b)$$

where the average wage gap is now written as the predicted gap due to differences in observable characteristics, the predicted gap due to whites' receipt of economic returns that exceed the population returns, and the predicted gap because the population returns exceed the economic returns of African Americans. The coefficients are based on pooled models and models estimated separately for African Americans and whites.

In these models, how does one simultaneously decompose the wage gap and account for the pre-market factors? The first decomposition could be constructed using OLS and including the AFQT score as a predictor variable. This is the typical approach in the literature. Taking advantage of the longitudinal structure of the NLSY might lead a researcher to estimate a fixed effect model by adding individual dummy variables. However, along with the person-specific fixed effect, all of the time invariant information (pre-market factors, years of schooling and race) would fall out of the equation. The next choice would be to estimate Equation (1) without the AFQT score using a random effects model. This model still treats the individual's effects as time-invariant, but it is now assumed to be random. The model's assumption that all of the predictor variables are uncorrelated with the person-specific effect may be too strong. For example, the individual effect, α_i may be correlated with years of schooling (Z_i) and race (R_i).

Hausman and Taylor's correlated random effects model provides a potential solution. Identification of both time-variant and time-invariant predictor variables is obtained by assuming that a subset of the time-variant predictor variables is correlated with the person-specific effect and some are not correlated. Instrumental variables for the predictor variables that are correlated with the person-specific effect must be constructed. To identify the first decomposition instruments are needed for education and race, while in the latter decomposition, an instrument for years of schooling is only needed because the models are estimated by race. Wilson and Ziliak use potential experience, state unemployment rates, and a dummy variable for southern residence as their instruments. Of their list of instruments, the state unemployment rate is the most plausible. I use the respondent's county unemployment rate. But I also construct instruments similar to the set used by Michael Boozer and colleagues (1992).[13] School desegregation did not begin in the South until after 1964 and the pace of change varied across states. This trend toward school desegregation should be correlated with years of schooling and race, but not with the time-invariant person-specific effect.

Unlike Boozer and colleagues' study, respondents in the NLSY were considerably younger. Our instrumental variable is based on whether the respondent started school prior to 1964. I create dummy variables that denote the respondent's state of residence at age 14 and interact these dummy variables with an indicator variable of whether the respondent started school prior to 1964. We still expect these instruments to be correlated with both education and race, but not the person-specific effect; however, the relation is contingent on the amount of moving that occurs between school entry and age fourteen.[12] (See Appendix Table 4C and 4D for state and regional NLSY data).

Table 4.5 presents the decomposition of the wage gap where discrimination is measured as the difference in intercepts. Column 1 constructs the decomposition using the OLS coefficients and including the AFQT score in the model. Column 2 constructs the decomposition using the OLS coefficients and excluding the AFQT score. Column 3 constructs the decomposition using the random effects coefficients and Column 4 constructs the decomposition using the coefficients from the correlated random effects model. The OLS results that include the AFQT score indicate that all but 2.3 percent the black-white wage gap among women can be explained and that an approximate 7 percent wage gap remains for men. The unexplained gap among women jumps to 10 percent if the AFQT is excluded and among men jumps to 15 percent. The random effects models have unexplained gaps that exceed the gap found in the OLS specification that includes the AFQT score.

In all four specifications, differences in the receipt of firm-provided training contribute little to the black-white wage gap. For women, these differences contribute 0.1 to 0.2 percentage points to the racial wage gap, while for men they contribute 0.1 to 0.5 percentage points. By comparison, differences in weeks of work experience contribute between 2 and 3 percentage points to the racial wage gap for women and between 3.7 and 4.5 points to the gap for men.

Table 4.6 presents the decomposition of the wage gap where discrimination is measured as the difference in returns to skill. Column 1 constructs the decomposition using the OLS coefficients and including the AFQT score. Column 2 constructs the decomposition using the OLS coefficients and excluding the AFQT score. Column 3 constructs the decomposition using the random effects coefficients and Column 4 constructs the decomposition using the coefficients from the correlated random effects model. The evidence in this table illustrates that the disadvantage to African Americans is in the form of economic returns that are below the population returns. With the exception of the correlated random effects model, the entries for white advantage are all basically zero. (See Appendix Tables 4E and 4F for OLS, random effects, and correlated random effects estimates from this analysis.)

SUMMARY AND CONCLUSIONS

The black-white wage remains an active area of research. Recent scholarship has responded to studies that find that much if not all of the gap can be attributed to racial differences in cognitive skills, as measured by AFQT scores. The new studies by William Spriggs and I (1996 and 2002), Patrick Mason (1997), and Arthur Goldsmith and colleagues (1998) find the existence of a large black-white wage gap, implying the need to refocus on the skills that African Americans acquire as adults in the labor market. A great deal of recent work also examines the role that on-the-job training plays in the labor market. This study reconnects the literature on racial wage gaps and on-the-job training. To do this, I use the NLSY, the most complete and comprehensive data set available on cognitive skills, work experience and training to examine the determinants of participation in training programs and estimate their ability to explain the black-white wage gap.

I further strengthen the correlated random effects model that Ziliak and Wilson estimate. I construct a new set of instruments by using the time series and cross state variation of whether the respondent started school prior to 1964, when mandated desegregation was begun in earnest. The quality of the instruments hinges on the amount of mobility that occurred (in state of residence) between the time the respondent first started school and the time he or she reached age 14. The wage analysis indicates that the correlated random effects model yields estimates of the black-white wage gap similar to those found by William Spriggs and me and by Beth Wilson and James Ziliak (1998). They are much larger than the estimates of the gap found by Derek Neal and William Johnson (1996). The gap among women ranges from 5.0 to 7.0 percent and among men from 11.0 to 11.5 percent. Racial differences in the AFQT score are much less important a determinant of the wage gap than Neal and Johnson found them to be.

As a result, research must shift its focus back to what happens in the workplace, especially with regard to understanding racial differences in the ability to build firm-specific or job-specific skills. The evidence presented shows that firms use company and seminar training programs most heavily for training young adults and also that these training programs are the most economically lucrative. These are the programs in which African Americans have lower participation rates than whites. Although differences in years of schooling explain the racial gap in company-based, in-house training, the racial gap in participation is not fully explained by differences in human capital, industry or geography.

There are several possible explanations for this training participation gap and each suggests a different direction for public policy. If the problem is lack of information or transportation, it suggests a greater focus on these elements in program design for both the public and private sector. If job segregation explains the gap in seminar training, then public policy should focus on insuring equal opportunity in all aspects of the employment relationship. The persistence of a significant, unexplained black-white wage gap underscores the need for this policy emphasis.

* * *

The author wishes to thank Berhanu Abegaz, Charles Betsy, Amy Crews, William Evans, Lawrence Katz, Lisa Lynch, Edward Montgomery, Yana Rodgers, William Spriggs, James Stewart, Kenneth Troske, Mark Turner, and Rhonda Williams for their helpful comments and suggestions on an earlier version of this paper. Steve McClaskie provided information on the content of the job training programs. Also deserving of thanks are the seminar participants at the U.S. Census Bureau's Center for Economic Studies, University of Maryland, Syracuse University, NEA/AEA Meetings in Washington, D.C., 1995, and the College of William and Mary for their comments on earlier versions of this paper.

TABLE 4.1
THE INCIDENCE OF FIRM-PROVIDED JOB TRAINING

Panel A: Women	White	(In Percent) African American	Difference
Company	8.8	8.6	0.2
Apprenticeship	0.0	0.2	-0.2
Business	0.5	0.5	0.0
Vocational	1.4	2.0	-0.6
Correspondence Course	0.4	0.2	0.2
Seminars Outside Work	4.2	1.5	2.6
Other Types	1.1	0.7	0.3

Panel B: Men	White	African American	Difference
Company	9.1	7.3	1.8
Apprenticeship	0.9	0.7	0.2
Business	0.3	0.6	-0.3
Vocational	1.4	1.4	0.1
Correspondence Course	0.5	0.3	0.2
Seminars Outside Work	3.0	0.9	2.1
Other Types	1.0	0.8	0.2

Notes: Authors' tabulations from the National Longitudinal Survey of Youth, 1988 to 1994. The samples consist of 3,651 white women-years, 1,680 African American women-years, 4,487 white men-years, and 1,992 African American men-years. Individuals are required to have completed their formal education by the 1988 interview and possess a complete set of information in each of the interviews from 1988 to 1994.

TABLE 4.2

FACTORS THAT AFFECT THE PROBABILITY OF TRAINING RECEIPT

	Women			Men			
	Company	Vocational	Seminar	Company	Apprenticeship	Vocational	Seminar
Worker Characteristics							
Years of Schooling	Positive & Significant	Negative, Not Significant	Positive & Significant	Positive & Significant	No Effect	Small Negative, but Significant	Small Positive but Significant
Actual Experience	No Effect	No Effect	No Effect	Small Positive but Significant	No Effect	No Effect	No Effect
Job Tenure	No Effect	Small, but Significant Negative Effect	Small, but Significant Positive Effect	No Effect	No Effect	Small negative, but Significant	No Effect
Union Membership	Positive, Not Significant	Positive, Not Significant	Positive, Not Significant	Positive, Not Significant	Small Positive, but Significant	Negative, Not Significant	Negative, Not Significant
Firm Characteristics							
Log (Firm Size)	Positive & Significant	Positive, Not Significant	Negative & Significant	Positive & Significant	No Effect	No Effect	No Effect
Public Sector	Positive, Not Significant	Negative, Not Significant	Negative, Not Significant	Positive, Not Significant	Small, Negative, But Significant	Positive, Not Significant	Negative, Not Significant
Location Characteristics							
Suburb (as compared with outside metro area)	Positive, Not Significant	Negative, Not Significant	Negative, Not Significant	Positive & Significant	Positive, Not Significant	No Effect	Positive, Significant
Central City (as compared with outside metro area)	Negative, Not Significant	Negative & Significant	Negative, Not Significant	Negative, Not Significant	Positive, Not Significant	No Effect	Negative, Not Significant
Local Area Unemployment Rate	Negative & Significant	Negative, Not Significant	Small Positive, But Significant	Positive, Not Significant	No Effect	Negative, Not Significant	No Effect

Notes: Summarizes results from probit analysis reported in Appendix Table.

TABLE 4.3

ECONOMIC RETURNS TO SCHOOLING, EXPERIENCE, TENURE, COGNITIVE SKILLS

	OLS with AFQT		OLS without AFQT		Random Effects		Correlated Random Effects	
	Women	Men	Women	Men	Women	Men	Women	Men
Panel A: African American								
Years of Schooling	4.30%	4.10%	6.70%	6.50%	7.30%	7.00%	6.20%	5.00%
Actual Experience (in Weeks)	0.02%	0.02%	0.02%	0.04%	0.06%	0.05%	0.03%	0.02%
Tenure (in Weeks)	0.12%	0.12%	0.10%	0.10%	0.11%	0.09%	0.11%	0.10%
Age-Adjusted AFQT	0.50%	0.50%	-	-	-	-	-	-
Panel B: White								
Years of Schooling	6.00%	5.70%	7.50%	7.50%	7.40%	7.50%	9.40%	9.40%
Actual Experience (in Weeks)	0.05%	0.05%	0.10%	0.10%	0.09%	0.08%	0.06%	0.08%
Tenure (in Weeks)	0.12%	0.08%	0.10%	0.10%	0.10%	0.07%	0.10%	0.06%
Age-Adjusted AFQT	0.20%	0.20%	—	—	—	—	—	—

Notes: Authors' tabulations from the National Longitudinal Survey of Youth, 1988 to 1991. Each entry is the percentage change in earnings generated by of a one unit change in the specified variable. The entries are the coefficients on years of schooling, actual experience, tenure at current job, and the AFQT score from earnings equations multiplied by 100. The models also include training, firm size, industry, public sector, region, marital status, metropolitan residence, union membership, local area unemployment rate and year dummy variables. All models include the square of actual experience and tenure. In the correlated random effects model, the instruments are the local area unemployment rate, dummy variables for state of residence at age 14, a dummy variable for whether the respondent started school prior to 1964, and interactions between the state dummy variables and the school start variable. The superscripts denote the level of significance: "a"-significant at the 1 percent level, "b"- significant at the 5 percent level, and "c" significant at the 10 percent level.

TABLE 4.4

PERCENTAGE CHANGE IN WORKER EARNINGS ASSOCIATED WITH FIRM PROVIDED TRAINING

	OLS with AFQT		OLS without AFQT		Random Effects		Correlated Random Effects	
	Women	Men	Women	Men	Women	Men	Women	Men
Panel A: African American								
Company	9.20%	7.80%	11.70%	11.60%	5.00%	6.70%	5.50%	10.50%
Apprenticeship	4.70%	3.40%	6.10%	7.40%	0.20%	8.20%	-1.40%	7.60%
Business School	-4.10%	4.10%	-1.90%	5.30%	-0.30%	1.30%	-0.90%	0.70%
Vocational	-3.60%	-4.90%	-2.40%	-3.20%	-3.90%	-7.20%	-3.60%	-7.90%
Correspondence	10.40%	-3.80%	12.50%	-6.60%	0.80%	-4.80%	2.00%	-3.00%
Seminar	7.30%	19.40%	8.40%	21.90%	-0.20%	13.30%	1.00%	17.40%
Other	21.00%	-5.60%	25.10%	-6.80%	18.40%	-5.70%	18.40%	-7.30%
Panel B: White								
Company	7.70%	11.90%	8.20%	13.00%	5.70%	8.60%	6.40%	10.00%
Apprenticeship	—	-10.40%	—	-8.80%	—	-6.60%	—	-5.30%
Business School	-4.50%	-7.70%	-5.00%	-5.40%	4.10%	-12.90%	3.10%	-14.80%
Vocational	-6.50%	1.80%	-5.80%	2.00%	-4.80%	0.90%	-4.90%	1.30%
Correspondence	-6.20%	-10.10%	-5.40%	-9.40%	-6.90%	-12.30%	-2.80%	-13.50%
Seminar	4.40%	12.90%	5.20%	14.10%	1.00%	8.90%	2.80%	11.20%
Other	-4.40%	-0.90%	-2.50%	-1.10%	-1.40%	2.20%	-1.70%	4.90%

Notes: Authors' tabulations from the National Longitudinal Survey of Youth, 1988 to 1991. Each entry is the percentage change in earnings associated with receipt of training of each type. The entries are the coefficients on training variables multiplied by 100. The models also include years of schooling, actual experience and job tenure, firm size, industry, public sector, region, marital status, metropolitan residence, union membership, local area unemployment rate and year dummy variables. All models include the square of actual experience and tenure. In the correlated random effects model, the instruments are the local area unemployment rate, dummy variables for state of residence at age 14, a dummy variable for whether the respondent started school prior to 1964, and interactions between the state dummy variables and the school start variable. The superscripts denote the level of significance: "a"-significant at the 1 percent level, "b"-significant at the 5 percent level, and "c"-significant at the 10 percent level.

TABLE 4.5

DECOMPOSITION OF BLACK-WHITE WAGE DIFFERENCES: DIFFERENCE IN INTERCEPTS

Variable	(1) OLS with AFQT		(2) OLS without AFQT		(3) Random Effects		(4) Correlated Random Effects	
	Women	Men	Women	Men	Women	Men	Women	Men
Total Gap in Percent	10.5	25.4	10.5	25.4	10.5	25.4	10.5	25.4
Due to Differences in Means	8.3	18.5	0.3	10.6	3.3	10.7	4.6	10.9
Years of Schooling	0.6	1.9	0.8	2.7	0.8	2.9	1.3	3.8
Actual Experience	2.3	3.7	2.3	3.8	3.0	4.4	3.0	4.5
Firm Size	-2.1	-1.2	-2.3	-1.2	-1.6	-0.6	-1.4	-0.1
Industry	-1.4	0.6	-1.4	0.5	-0.6	0.2	-0.4	0.6
Public	1.1	0.3	1.2	0.4	0.4	0.0	0.6	-0.2
Region	1.6	2.0	2.0	2.2	2.2	1.8	2.6	1.0
Married	0.3	2.1	0.5	2.1	0.4	1.5	0.3	1.0
Metropolitan	-1.6	-0.8	-1.8	-0.9	-0.8	-0.5	-0.6	-0.4
Union	-1.1	-1.2	-0.9	-1.1	-0.5	-0.8	-0.8	-1.3
Tenure	0.1	1.5	0.1	1.6	0.1	1.4	0.0	1.2
Unemployment rate	-0.4	-0.4	-0.4	-0.5	-0.2	-0.2	-0.1	-0.1
Training	0.2	0.4	0.2	0.5	0.1	0.1	0.1	0.2
Year	0.2	0.4	0.2	0.4	0.4	0.6	0.5	0.6
AFQT	8.7	9.1	na	na	na	na	na	na
Health Status	0.0	0.0	0.0	0.0	0.0	0.0	0.0	0.0
Number of Jobs	-0.3	0.1	-0.3	0.0	-0.3	0.1	-0.5	0.1
Individual Effect	na	na	na	na	na	na	na	na
Unexplained Gap	2.3	7.0	10.2	14.9	6.3	15.1	2.9	16.0

Notes: Authors' tabulations from the National Longitudinal Survey of Youth, 1988 to 1994. The entries are the contribution in percentage points of a variable to the black-white wage gap.

TABLE 4.6

DECOMPOSITION OF BLACK-WHITE WAGE GAP
DISCRIMINATION AS DIFFERENCES IN RETURNS-TO-SKILL

Variable	(1) OLS with AFQT		(2) OLS without AFQT		(3) Random Effects		(4) Correlated Random Effects	
	Women	Men	Women	Men	Women	Men	Women	Men
Total Gap in Percent	10.5	25.4	10.5	25.4	10.5	25.4	10.5	25.4
Due to Differences in Means	8.3	18.5	0.3	10.6	3.3	10.7	6.6	11.3
African-American Disadvantage	2.3	7.0	10.2	14.9	6.2	15.1	4.8	9.6
White Advantage	0.0	0.0	0.0	0.0	0.1	0.1	2.6	4.6

Notes: Authors' tabulations from the National Longitudinal Survey of Youth, 1988 to 1994. Appendix Table A5 presents more detailed results.

APPENDIX TABLE 4A

PROBIT ESTIMATES OF
THE DETERMINANTS OF TRAINING BY TYPE

Panel A: Women	Black	White	Company Coef.	Company dP/dX	Vocational Coef.	Vocational dP/dX	Seminar Coef.	Seminar dP/dX
Worker Characteristics								
Black = 1			-0.042	-0.006	0.235^b	0.008	-0.289^a	-0.014
Years of Schooling	12.91	13.02	0.048^a	0.007	-0.027	-0.001	0.099^a	0.005
Actual Experience								
(in Weeks)	438	482	0.000	0.000	0.000	0.000	0.000	0.000
Union = 1	0.25	0.11	0.018	0.003	0.060	0.002	-0.098	-0.005
Tenure (In Weeks)	212	210	0.000	0.000	-0.001^c	0.000	0.002^a	0.000
Married = 1	0.38	0.65	0.018	0.003	-0.031	-0.001	0.007	0.000
Separated = 1	0.08	0.03	-0.149	-0.020	-0.419	-0.009	0.184	0.011
Divorced = 1	0.10	0.13	-0.024	-0.004	0.271	0.011	0.111	0.006
Remarried = 1	0.01	0.00	-0.512^c	-0.051	0.436	0.022	0.191	0.012
Firm Characteristics								
Log(Firm Size)	4.89	4.07	0.052^a	0.008	0.012	0.000	-0.037^a	-0.002
Mining = 1	0.00	0.00	.	.	.	.	0.299	0.021
Construction = 1	0.00	0.01	0.343	0.062	5.066^a	0.986	0.091	0.005
Manufacturing = 1	0.18	0.18	0.513	0.093	4.566^a	0.929	-0.124	-0.006
Transportation, Comm.,								
and Pub. Util.=1	0.04	0.05	0.910	0.218	4.237^a	0.955	0.337	0.024
Wholesale and								
Retail Trade=1	0.19	0.24	0.437	0.075	4.494^a	0.891	-0.368	-0.016
Finance, Insurance								
and Real Estate = 1	0.08	0.10	0.767	0.165	4.428^a	0.955	0.159	0.009
Business and Repair								
Services = 1	0.07	0.05	0.558	0.112	4.423^a	0.966	0.116	0.007
Personal Services = 1	0.06	0.04	0.449	0.085	4.238^a	0.955	0.030	0.002
Entertainment and								
Recreation Services = 1	0.01	0.01	0.358	0.066	4.349^a	0.969	-0.081	-0.004
Professional and								
Related Services = 1	0.24	0.25	0.667	0.122	4.437^a	0.855	0.297	0.018
Public Administration = 1	0.12	0.04	0.949^b	0.227	4.458^a	0.966	0.282	0.019
Public = 1	0.25	0.13	0.112	0.017	-0.051	-0.002	-0.006	0.000
Location Characteristics								
Midwest = 1	0.16	0.34	0.147^a	0.022	0.239	0.008	0.068	0.004
South = 1	0.66	0.34	-0.017	-0.002	0.004	0.000	-0.069	-0.004
West = 1	0.05	0.15	0.172^b	0.027	0.091	0.003	0.195	0.012
Suburb = 1	0.25	0.37	0.011	0.002	-0.093	-0.003	-0.039	-0.002
Suburb, Central City								
not known = 1	0.37	0.30	0.039	0.006	-0.094	-0.003	-0.089	-0.004
Central City = 1	0.22	0.07	-0.017	-0.002	-0.537^a	-0.011	-0.094	-0.005
Local Area								
Unemployment Rate	6.08	6.39	-0.036^a	-0.005	-0.006	0.000	0.031^a	0.002
Constant			-2.718		-6.112		-3.446	
Observed Probability (P)			0.088		0.016		0.033	

Notes: Authors' tabulations from the National Longitudinal Survey of Youth, 1988 to 1994. The entries are probit coefficients, followed by the probability effect. All models include the square of actual experience and tenure and year dummy variables. The excluded groups are agriculture, private sector, north, never married, non-metropolitan, non-union member, and the year dummy variable for 1988. The superscripts denote the level of significance: "a"-significant at the 1 percent level, "b"- significant at the 5 percent level, and "c" significant at the 10 percent level.

APPENDIX TABLE 4A (CONT'D)

Panel B: Men	Black Mean	White Mean	Company Coef.	Company dP/dX	Apprentice-ship Coef.	Apprentice-ship dP/dX	Vocational Coef.	Vocational dP/dX	Seminar Coef.	Seminar dP/dX
Worker Characteristics										
Black = 1			-0.071	-0.009	-0.109	-0.001	0.007	0.000	-0.362ª	-0.011
Years of Schooling	12.32	12.69	0.100ª	0.013	0.000	0.000	-0.053ª	-0.001	0.090ª	0.003
Actual Experience (in Weeks)	444	501	0.002ª	0.000	0.001	0.000	0.001	0.000	-0.002	0.000
Union = 1	0.25	0.08	0.055	0.007	0.541ª	0.006	-0.054	-0.002	-0.028	-0.001
Tenure (In Weeks)	0.27	0.18	0.000	0.000	-0.002	0.000	-0.003ª	0.000	0.000	0.000
Married = 1	0.39	0.62	0.134ª	0.017	-0.046	-0.001	0.088	0.002	0.271ª	0.009
Separated = 1	0.06	0.03	0.082	0.011	—	—	0.120	0.004	0.123	0.005
Divorced = 1	0.06	0.09	0.109	0.015	-0.093	-0.001	0.324ᵇ	0.013	-0.085	-0.003
Firm Characteristics										
Log(Firm Size)	4.40	3.83	0.056ª	0.007	-0.015	0.000	0.010	0.000	-0.024	-0.001
Mining = 1	0.00	0.01	0.442	0.078	—	—	0.216	0.008	1.142	0.126
Construction = 1	0.13	0.14	0.148	0.021	—	—	0.173	0.006	0.222	0.009
Manufacturing = 1	0.24	0.28	0.646ª	0.105	0.414	0.007	0.285	0.009	0.678	0.035
Transportation, Comm., and Pub. Util.=1	0.10	0.08	0.785ª	0.159	0.255	0.003	0.087	0.003	0.591	0.035
Wholesale and Retail Trade=1	0.18	0.20	0.696ª	0.123	0.146	0.002	0.194	0.006	0.611	0.033
Finance, Insurance and Real Estate = 1	0.04	0.04	0.768ª	0.160	-0.412	-0.003	0.260	0.010	1.083	0.108
Business and Repair Services = 1	0.08	0.07	0.677ª	0.131	0.093	0.001	0.440	0.019	0.743	0.052
Personal Services = 1	0.03	0.02	0.136	0.019	0.329	0.005	-0.139	-0.003	0.980	0.092
Entertainment and Recreation Services = 1	0.01	0.01	0.257	0.040	-0.024	0.000	0.095	0.003	0.353	0.018
Professional and Related Services = 1	0.09	0.06	0.491ᶜ	0.086	0.288	0.004	0.389	0.016	0.950	0.080
Public Administration = 1	0.07	0.05	0.891ª	0.195	-0.055	-0.001	0.568	0.029	0.951	0.083
Public = 1	0.18	0.11	0.166	0.024	-0.428ª	-0.003	0.036	0.001	-0.048	-0.002
Location Characteristics										
Midwest = 1	0.15	0.37	0.086	0.011	0.150	0.002	0.155	0.005	0.314ª	0.013
South = 1	0.64	0.31	0.003	0.000	0.086	0.001	-0.142	-0.004	0.223ᵇ	0.008
West = 1	0.07	0.16	0.117	0.016	0.215	0.003	0.106	0.003	0.248ᶜ	0.011
Suburb = 1	0.00	0.00	0.147ª	0.020	0.193	0.002	-0.006	0.000	0.266ª	0.010
Suburb, Central City not known = 1	0.19	0.38	0.089	0.012	0.346ᶜ	0.005	-0.053	-0.001	0.073	0.003
Central City = 1	0.36	0.26	-0.024	-0.003	0.086	0.001	-0.010	0.000	-0.041	-0.001
Local Area Unemployment Rate	6.02	6.54	0.007	0.001	0.009	0.000	-0.022	-0.001	-0.011	0.000
Constant			-4.189		-2.712		-1.413		-3.803	
Observed Probability (P)			0.085		0.009		0.014		0.023	

Notes: Authors' tabulations from the National Longitudinal Survey of Youth, 1988 to 1994. The entries are probit coefficients, followed by the probability effect. All models include the square of actual experience and tenure and year dummy variables. The excluded groups are agriculture, private sector, north, never married, non-metropolitan, non-union member, and the year dummy variable for 1988. The superscripts denote the level of significance: "a"-significant at the 1 percent level, "b"- significant at the 5 percent level, and "c" significant at the 10 percent level.

APPENDIX TABLE 4B

RETURNS TO SCHOOLING, EXPERIENCE, TENURE, COGNITIVE SKILLS AND FIRM PROVIDED TRAINING

Panel A:	OLS with AFQT		OLS without AFQT		Random Effects		Correlated Random Effects	
African American	Women	Men	Women	Men	Women	Men	Women	Men
Years of Schooling	0.043[a]	0.041[a]	0.067[a]	0.065[a]	0.073[a]	0.070[a]	0.062[b]	0.050[b]
Actual Experience (in Weeks)	0.0002	0.0002	0.0002	0.0004	0.0006[c]	0.0005	0.0003[b]	0.0002
Tenure (in Weeks)	0.0012[a]	0.0012	0.001[a]	0.001[a]	0.0011[a]	0.0009[a]	0.0011	0.0010
Company	0.092[a]	0.078[c]	0.117[a]	0.116[a]	0.050[c]	0.067	0.055	0.105[a]
Apprenticeship	0.047	0.034	0.061	0.074	0.002	0.082	-0.014	0.076
Business School	-0.041	0.041	-0.019	0.053	-0.003	0.013	-0.009	0.007
Vocational	-0.036	-0.049	-0.024	-0.032	-0.039	-0.072	-0.036	-0.079
Correspondence	0.104	-0.038	0.125	-0.066	0.008	-0.048	0.020	-0.030
Seminar	0.073	0.194[c]	0.084	0.219[c]	-0.002	0.133	0.010	0.174
Other	0.210[c]	-0.056	0.251	-0.068	0.184[b]	-0.057	0.184[b]	-0.073
Age-Adjusted AFQT	0.005[a]	0.005[a]	-	-	-	-	-	-
Panel B: White								
Years of Schooling	0.060[a]	0.057[a]	0.075[a]	0.075[a]	0.074[a]	0.075[a]	0.094[a]	0.094[a]
Actual Experience (in Weeks)	0.0005	0.0005	0.001[c]	0.001	0.0009[b]	0.0008[c]	0.0006	0.0008[c]
Tenure (in Weeks)	0.0012	0.0008	0.001[a]	0.001[a]	0.0010[a]	0.0007[a]	0.0010[a]	0.0006[a]
Company	0.077[a]	0.119[a]	0.082[a]	0.130[a]	0.057[b]	0.086[a]	0.064[b]	0.100[a]
Apprenticeship	.	-0.104	.	-0.088	.	-0.066	.	-0.053
Business School	-0.045	-0.077	-0.050	-0.054	0.041	-0.129	0.031	-0.148
Vocational	-0.065	0.018	-0.058	0.020	-0.048	0.009	-0.049	0.013
Correspondence	-0.062	-0.101	-0.054	-0.094	-0.069	-0.123	-0.028	-0.135
Seminar	0.044	0.129[a]	0.052	0.141[a]	0.010	0.089[b]	0.028	0.112[a]
Other	-0.044	-0.009	-0.025	-0.011	-0.014	0.022	-0.017	0.049
Age-Adjusted AFQT	0.002[a]	0.002[a]	-	-	-	-	-	-

Notes: Authors' tabulations from the National Longitudinal Survey of Youth, 1988 to 1991. The entries are the coefficients on years of schooling, actual experience, tenure at current job, the AFQT Score and training from earnings equations. The models also include firm size, industry, public sector, region, marital status, metropolitan residence, union membership, local area unemployment rate and year dummy variables. All models include the square of actual experience and tenure. In the correlated random effects model, the instruments are the local area unemployment rate, dummy variables for state of residence at age 14, a dummy variable for whether the respondent started school prior to 1964, and interactions between the state dummy variables and the school start variable. The superscripts denote the level of significance: "a"-significant at the 1 percent level, "b"- significant at the 5 percent level, and "c" significant at the 10 percent level.

APPENDIX TABLE 4C

RESIDENCE AT AGE 14 BY WHETHER RESPONDENT STARTED SCHOOL BEFORE 1964

| | Women | | | | Men | | | |
| | African American | | White | | African American | | White | |
State	Post-1964	Pre-1964	Post-1964	Pre-1964	Post-1964	Pre-1964	Post-1964	Pre-1964
CT	9	4	14	10	9	3	9	0
ME	0	0	1	0	0	0	0	0
MA	6	0	17	3	11	0	17	4
NH	0	0	0	2	0	0	3	0
NY	64	27	195	46	137	13	211	38
PA	49	14	216	41	44	20	258	32
RI	0	4	0	0	0	0	0	0
VT	0	0	3	2	0	0	0	0
NJ	49	8	157	31	51	24	201	25
IL	35	7	86	22	53	12	156	29
IN	6	0	80	6	30	0	108	15
IA	0	0	71	4	2	0	69	6
KS	0	0	18	4	4	0	32	7
MI	37	4	205	37	42	8	264	38
MN	0	0	135	6	0	0	153	13
MO	30	0	72	6	57	8	100	10
NE	8	0	17	0	0	2	13	18
ND	0	0	4	0	0	0	0	3
OH	99	6	231	62	51	9	316	52
SD	0	0	10	0	0	0	28	0
WI	13	0	182	30	15	8	229	60
AL	123	10	91	3	141	15	133	20
AR	20	9	23	8	53	16	26	8
DE	0	0	5	0	0	0	4	0
DC	44	3	6	0	70	4	0	0
FL	95	8	94	34	56	5	100	7
GA	164	27	29	9	230	30	89	14
KY	3	0	14	0	0	0	11	0
LA	18	4	23	0	27	4	8	0
MD	24	8	24	4	10	0	41	22
MS	45	11	20	2	33	4	12	1
NC	101	11	164	37	138	12	177	46
OK	16	2	43	14	28	4	40	24
SC	141	27	41	9	135	8	31	8
TN	15	4	101	19	10	0	108	10
TX	102	12	123	18	125	15	80	35
VA	60	3	35	12	97	12	116	20
WV	12	0	89	7	4	0	99	7

Notes: Author's tabulations from the NLSY. To be included in the sample, respondents were required to have a complete set of information firm size, industry, public sector, region, marital status, metropolitan residence, union membership, local area unemployment rate, the eight types of training, actual experience, tenure at current job, age-adjusted AFQT score, and years of schooling.

APPENDIX TABLE 4C (CONT'D.)

State	Women African American Post-1964	Pre-1964	White Post-1964	Pre-1964	Men African American Post-1964	Pre-1964	White Post-1964	Pre-1964
AK	0	0	10	4	3	0	13	10
AZ	0	0	16	0	7	0	32	13
CA	66	6	216	8	68	12	232	45
CO	0	0	62	13	0	0	65	13
HI	4	0	0	0	0	0	4	3
ID	0	0	0	0	0	0	3	0
MT	0	0	29	11	0	0	56	7
NV	0	0	0	0	0	0	5	0
NM	3	0	9	4	0	0	6	6
OR	0	0	7	4	0	0	21	11
UT	0	0	2	3	3	0	3	0
WA	0	0	53	14	0	0	42	7
WY	0	0	2	0	0	0	4	0
Total	1461	219	3045	549	1744	248	3728	687
South(Freq)	983	139	925	176	1157	129	1075	222
South(%)	67%	63%	30%	32%	66%	52%	29%	32%

Notes: Author's tabulations from the NLSY. To be included in the sample, respondents were required to have a complete set of information firm size, industry, public sector, region, marital status, metropolitan residence, union membership, local area unemployment rate, the eight types of training, actual experience, tenure at current job, age-adjusted AFQT score, and years of schooling.

APPENDIX TABLE 4D

Respondents that Started School Prior to 1964

Number	Women African American	White	Men African American	White
Total	219	549	248	687
South	139	176	129	222
Percent				
Total	13%	15%	12%	16%
South	12%	16%	10%	17%

Notes: Figures represent number and share of respondents that were enrolled in school prior to 1964.

APPENDIX TABLE 4E: OLS, RANDOM EFFECTS, AND CORRELATED RANDOM EFFECTS ESTIMATES OF THE BLACK-WHITE WAGE GAP: DISCRIMINATION AS DIFFERENCE IN RETURNS-TO-SKILL

Variable	OLS with AFQT Women	Men	OLS without AFQT Women	Men	Random Effects Women	Men	Correlated Random Effects Women	Men
Total Gap	0.105	0.254	0.105	0.254	0.105	0.254	0.105	0.254
Due to Differences in Means	0.083	0.185	0.003	0.106	0.033	0.107	0.066	0.113
Education	0.006	0.019	0.008	0.027	0.008	0.029	0.013	0.044
Actual Experience	0.023	0.037	0.023	0.038	0.030	0.044	0.034	0.069
Firm Size	-0.021	-0.012	-0.023	-0.012	-0.016	-0.006	-0.014	-0.004
Industry	-0.014	0.006	-0.014	0.005	-0.006	0.002	-0.004	0.001
Public	0.011	0.003	0.012	0.004	0.004	0.000	0.002	-0.002
Region	0.016	0.020	0.020	0.022	0.022	0.018	0.029	-0.013
Marital Status	0.003	0.021	0.005	0.021	0.004	0.015	0.004	0.006
Metropolitan	-0.016	-0.008	-0.018	-0.009	-0.008	-0.005	0.002	-0.004
Union	-0.011	-0.012	-0.009	-0.011	-0.005	-0.008	-0.003	-0.007
Tenure	0.001	0.015	0.001	0.016	0.001	0.014	0.000	0.013
Unemployment Rate	-0.004	-0.004	-0.004	-0.005	-0.002	-0.002	-0.001	-0.001
Training	0.002	0.004	0.002	0.005	0.001	0.001	0.001	0.000
Year	0.002	0.004	0.002	0.004	0.004	0.006	0.005	0.010
AFQT	0.087	0.091						
Health	0.000	0.000	0.000	0.000	0.000	0.000	0.000	0.000
Number of jobs	-0.003	0.001	-0.003	0.000	-0.003	0.001	-0.002	0.000
Individual effect	na	na	na	na	0.009	-0.005	-0.035	-0.001
African American Disadvantage	0.023	0.070	0.102	0.149	0.062	0.151	0.048	0.096
Education	0.123	0.181	0.062	0.111	0.007	0.056	0.239	-0.391
Actual Experience	-0.035	0.041	-0.026	0.054	-0.003	0.076	-0.010	0.563
Firm Size	0.040	0.002	0.040	0.001	0.001	-0.006	-0.006	-0.001
Industry	-0.162	0.115	-0.223	0.133	-0.167	0.069	-0.168	0.038
Public	-0.008	-0.014	-0.007	-0.013	0.000	-0.009	0.001	-0.007
Region	0.043	0.050	0.052	0.057	0.037	0.039	-0.022	0.056
Marital Status	-0.001	0.002	-0.004	0.001	-0.003	-0.011	0.000	-0.010
Metropolitan	0.044	0.073	0.038	0.063	0.015	0.038	-0.024	0.022
Union	-0.001	0.003	-0.003	0.005	0.000	0.005	0.002	0.008
Tenure	-0.006	-0.041	-0.008	-0.045	-0.029	-0.030	-0.031	-0.024
Unemployment Rate	-0.071	0.097	-0.050	0.108	-0.027	0.065	-0.025	0.038
Training	-0.001	0.000	-0.003	-0.003	-0.001	-0.001	0.000	0.001
Year	0.004	0.011	0.004	0.006	-0.001	0.005	0.001	-0.111
AFQT	0.027	0.038	-	-	-	-	-	-
Health	0.001	-0.001	0.001	-0.001	0.000	0.000	0.000	0.000
Number of jobs	-0.020	-0.020	-0.038	-0.020	-0.049	-0.031	-0.069	-0.080
Constant	0.049	-0.469	0.266	-0.309	0.282	-0.115	0.160	-0.006
White Advantage	0.000	0.000	0.000	0.000	0.001	0.001	0.026	0.046
Education	0.056	0.084	0.019	0.042	0.002	0.004	0.053	-0.431
Actual Experience	-0.032	0.034	-0.024	0.044	-0.014	0.079	-0.031	0.860
Firm Size	0.015	0.003	0.015	0.004	-0.002	-0.002	-0.005	-0.004
Industry	-0.020	0.036	-0.023	0.038	-0.018	0.016	-0.013	0.004
Public	-0.003	-0.007	-0.003	-0.007	0.000	-0.004	0.001	-0.003
Region	0.017	0.015	0.019	0.017	0.010	0.014	-0.016	0.034
Marital Status	-0.006	0.005	-0.006	0.006	-0.008	-0.007	-0.007	-0.008
Metropolitan	0.009	0.026	0.008	0.024	-0.003	0.015	-0.005	0.016
Union	-0.002	0.001	-0.002	0.001	0.000	0.003	0.001	0.005
Tenure	-0.008	-0.022	-0.010	-0.023	-0.017	-0.013	-0.021	-0.014
Unemployment Rate	-0.020	0.036	-0.015	0.039	-0.015	0.024	-0.013	0.019
Training	-0.001	0.000	-0.002	-0.001	0.000	0.001	0.000	0.001
Year	0.002	0.005	0.002	0.003	0.002	-0.001	0.009	-0.174
AFQT	-0.006	-0.006						
Health	0.000	0.000	0.000	0.000	0.000	0.000	0.000	0.000
Number of Jobs	-0.013	-0.004	-0.018	-0.004	-0.024	-0.011	-0.048	-0.014
Constant	0.013	-0.206	0.040	-0.183	0.087	-0.116	0.121	-0.246

Notes: Authors' tabulations from the National Longitudinal Survey of Youth, 1988 to 1994. The entries are the contribution in log points of a variable to the black-white wage gap.

APPENDIX TABLE 4F

OLS, RANDOM EFFECTS, AND CORRELATED RANDOM EFFECTS ESTIMATES OF THE BLACK-WHITE WAGE GAP: DISCRIMINATION AS DIFFERENCE IN INTERCEPTS

Variable	OLS with AFQT		OLS without AFQT		Random Effects		Correlated Random Effects	
	Women	Men	Women	Men	Women	Men	Women	Men
Total Gap	0.105	0.254	0.105	0.254	0.105	0.254	0.105	0.254
Differences Due to Means	0.083	0.185	0.003	0.106	0.033	0.107	0.046	0.109
Years of Schooling	0.006	0.019	0.008	0.027	0.008	0.029	0.013	0.038
Actual Experience	0.023	0.037	0.023	0.038	0.030	0.044	0.030	0.045
Firm Size	-0.021	-0.012	-0.023	-0.012	-0.016	-0.006	-0.014	-0.001
Industry	-0.014	0.006	-0.014	0.005	-0.006	0.002	-0.004	0.006
Public	0.011	0.003	0.012	0.004	0.004	0.000	0.006	-0.002
Region	0.016	0.020	0.020	0.022	0.022	0.018	0.026	0.010
Married	0.003	0.021	0.005	0.021	0.004	0.015	0.003	0.010
Metropolitan	-0.016	-0.008	-0.018	-0.009	-0.008	-0.005	-0.006	-0.004
Union	-0.011	-0.012	-0.009	-0.011	-0.005	-0.008	-0.008	-0.013
Tenure	0.001	0.015	0.001	0.016	0.001	0.014	0.000	0.012
Unemployment Rate	-0.004	-0.004	-0.004	-0.005	-0.002	-0.002	-0.001	-0.001
Training	0.002	0.004	0.002	0.005	0.001	0.001	0.001	0.002
Year	0.002	0.004	0.002	0.004	0.004	0.006	0.005	0.006
AFQT	0.087	0.091	na	na	na	na	na	na
Health Status	0.000	0.000	0.000	0.000	0.000	0.000	0.000	0.000
Number of Jobs	-0.003	0.001	-0.003	0.000	-0.003	0.001	-0.005	0.001
Individual Effect	na	na	na	na	0.009	-0.004	0.030	-0.014
Unexplained	0.023	0.070	0.102	0.149	0.063	0.151	0.029	0.160

Notes: Authors' tabulations from the National Longitudinal Survey of Youth, 1988 to 1994. The entries are the contribution in log points of a variable to the black-white wage gap.

NOTES

1. John Bound and Richard B. Freeman, "What Went Wrong? The Erosion of Relative Earnings and Employment Among Young Black Men in the 1980's," *The Quarterly Journal of Economics* 107 (February 1992); Chinhui Juhn, Kevin Murphy, and Brooks Pierce, "Accounting for the Slowdown in Black-White Wage Convergence," in *Workers and Their Wages: Changing Patterns in the United States*, edited by M. Kosters (Washington, DC: AEI Press, 1991); William M. Rodgers III, "Male Black-White Wage Gaps, 1979-1991: A Distributional Analysis," (unpublished paper, The College of William and Mary, 1997), and "Male Sub-metropolitan Black-White Wage Gaps: New Evidence for the 1980s," *Urban Studies* 34 (1997). William M. Rodgers and William E. Spriggs, "Accounting for the Racial Gap in AFQT Scores: Comment on Nan L. Maxwell, 'The Effect on Black-White Wage Differences of Differences in the Quantity and Quality of Education'," *Industrial and Labor Relations Review*, vol. 55, no. 3 (2002): 533-541.

2. Derek A. Neal and William R. Johnson, "The Role of Pre-Market Factors in Black-White Differences," *The Journal of Political Economy* 104 (1996). N. Maxwell, "The Effect on Black-White Wage Differences of Differences in the Quantity and Quality of Education," *Industrial and Labor Relations Review* 47 (January 1994); Ronald F. Ferguson, "New Evidence on the Growing Value of Skill and Consequences for Racial Disparity and Returns to Schooling," (unpublished paper, John F. Kennedy School of Government, Harvard University, September 1994), and "Shifting Challenges: Fifty Years of Economic Change Toward Black-White Earnings Equality," *Daedalus* 124 (Winter 1995); and June O'Neill, "The Role of Human Capital in Earnings Differences Between Black and White Men," *The Journal of Economic Perspectives* 4 (1990).

3. William M. Rodgers III and William E. Spriggs, "What Does the AFQT Really Measure: Race, Wages, Schooling and the AFQT Score," *The Review of Black Political Economy* 24 (1996).

4. Arthur H Goldsmith, William Darity Jr., and Jonathan R Veum, "Race, Cognitive Skills, Psychological Capital, and Wages," *Review of Black Political Economy*, vol. 26, no. 2 (Fall 1998): 9-21. Patrick L. Mason, "Race, Culture, and Skill: Interracial Wage Differences among African Americans, Latinos, and Whites," *The Review of Black Political Economy*, Winter 1997.

5. William M. Rodgers III and William E. Spriggs, "Accounting for the Racial Gap in AFQT Scores: Comment on Nan L. Maxwell, 'The Effect on Black-White Wage Differences of Differences in the Quantity and Quality of Education' " (*Industrial and Labor Relations Review*, vol. 55, no. 3 (2002)).

6. Greg J. Duncan and Saul Hoffman, "On-the-Job Training and Earnings Differences by Race and Sex," *Review of Economics and Statistics* 61 (November 1979).

7. Mary Corcoran, and Greg J. Duncan. "Work History, Labor Force Attachment, and Earnings Differences Between the Races and Sexes." *The Journal of Human Resources* 14 (1979).

8. Edwin A. Sexton and Reed N. Olsen, "The Returns to On-the-Job Training: Are They the same for Blacks and Whites?" *The Southern Economic Journal* 61 (October 1994).

9. Veum, 1995; Lisa M. Lynch, "Private-Sector Training and the Earnings of Young Workers," American Economic Review 82 (1992).

10. We exclude the military sample. Doing this reduces the sample to 1,280. Along

with a stratified random sample, the National Longitudinal Survey of Youth over-samples low-income whites, blacks and Hispanics. In 1990, the low-income whites were dropped from the sample. Respondents used in this study are from the stratified random sample or the low-income black and Hispanic samples.

11. The interval in the 1988 interview covers 1986 to 1988. The intervals for the 1989, 1990 and 1991 interviews cover the preceding year.

12. Beth A. Wilson and James P. Ziliak, "Pre-Market Factors and the Black-White Wage Gap: Evidence from Panel Data" (unpublished manuscript, Xavier University and University of Oregon, 1998).

13. Michael A. Boozer, Alan B. Krueger, and Shari Wolkon, "Race and School Quality since *Brown* v. *Board of Education*," Brookings Papers on Economic Activity (Microeconomics) (1992): 269-326.

14. As a preliminary check on the quality of our instruments, I regressed years of schooling on these variables plus the local area unemployment rate. The F-statistic for women is 6.78 and 11.46 for men. Both are well above the 1 percent level of significance. The corresponding R^2s are 0.10 and 0.14. The F-statistics from regressions of the dummy variable that equals 1 if the respondent is African American, and 0 if the respondent is white indicate the presence of quite a strong relation. The F-statistics for the female and male regressions are 20.52 and 25.53, well above the 1 percent level of significance. The R^2s are both 0.26.

Chapter Five

DO BLACK WORKERS LACK SOFT SKILLS?

Cecilia A. Conrad

INTRODUCTION

Recent surveys suggest that employers have negative perceptions of the soft skills of urban minority workers, particularly young African American males.[1] These findings are alarming because many employers of entry-level workers cite soft skills as important criteria in their hiring decisions.[2] If African American workers lack soft skills or if employers perceive that they do, this could be a significant obstacle to employment in the 21st century.

This paper explores whether African Americans lack soft skills relative to other entry-level workers and examines the implications for employment policy. Any evaluation of the significance of soft skills as an employment obstacle requires, first, a precise definition of soft skills; second, some tools for the skills' assessment; and third, an appraisal of the skills' importance in the hiring decision. The first section of this paper presents a precise definition of soft skills, representing a synthesis of colloquial usage and published references, and then discusses current problems with assessment. The second section summarizes the evidence that there is a racial gap in soft skills and examines the impact of this gap (real or perceived) on African American employment. The third section describes selected soft skills training programs and reviews their effectiveness, and the final section suggests directions for public policy.

The principal findings are as follows:

- Soft skills are inherently difficult to assess. This creates an environment conducive to statistical discrimination. Employers tend to rely on signals of a worker's soft skills including stereotyped attributes such as race or neighborhood, as well as observed behavior in personal interviews.

- The evidence that black workers lack soft skills relative to other workers is largely impressionistic. A substantial minority of employers perceives a deficit, but this perception has not been corroborated or refuted with direct assessments.

- Appropriate remedies for soft skills deficits (real and perceived) must not only assist workers in acquiring the soft skills they need, but must also address employers' need for a credible assessment of those skills.

WHAT ARE SOFT SKILLS?

Soft skills are nontechnical skills, abilities, and traits required to function in a specific employment environment so as to (1) deliver information and services to customers and coworkers; (2) work effectively as a member of a team; (3) learn or acquire the technical skills required to perform tasks; (4) inspire the confidence of supervisors and management; and (5) understand and adapt to the cultural norms of the workplace.[3] The Joint Center developed this definition following a careful survey of existing usage and interviews with job training experts. Table 5.1 provides a taxonomy. Soft skills include practical cognition or problem-solving skills, verbal communication skills, and interpersonal and teamwork skills, as well as personal qualities and work ethic.

Success in the labor market clearly requires more than competence in the technical aspects of a job. For example, information systems managers are looking for programmers who can not only write code but also communicate with users.[4] Business schools have added soft skills courses to their MBA curricula.[5] DeVry Institute, a commercially operated chain of vocational schools, requires electronic technicians to take courses in human relations and teamwork.[6] In a comprehensive effort to identify generic skills required of all workers, the U.S. Secretary of Labor's Commission on Achieving Necessary Skills (SCANS) identified a three-part basic foundation and five workplace competencies.[7] In addition to the traditional three R's (reading, writing and arithmetic), SCANS' three-part basic foundation includes basic listening and speaking skills, thinking skills, and personal qualities such as individual responsibility, self-esteem, integrity, and sociability. Two other national inventories of skill requirements offer similar findings. The National Academy of Sciences[8] asked a panel of employers to assess the skills required of high school graduates who enter the work force immediately after graduation. Leading the employer's list were oral communication skills, interpersonal skills, and work habits. The American Society for Training and Development's (ASTD's) nationwide survey of employers yielded similar results.[9] (Employers want workers with communication and adaptability skills (problem-solving and thinking creatively); group effectiveness skills (interpersonal skills, teamwork, negotiation); influencing skills (understanding organizational culture, sharing leadership); and development skills (self-esteem, motivation and goal setting, career development). In a survey by Philip Moss and Chris Tilley, 86 percent of employers included soft skills in their list of most important hiring criteria.[10]

TABLE 5.1

SOFT SKILLS TAXONOMY

Practical Cognition

- Identifies problems
- Considers and evaluates alternative solutions, weighing their risks and benefits
- Formulates and reaches decisions logically
- Separates fact from opinion
- Adjusts to unanticipated situations by applying established rules and facts
- Works out new ways of handling recurring problems
- Determines what is needed to accomplish work assignments

Oral Communication Skills

- Communicates in oral messages appropriate to listeners and situations
- Understands and gives instructions
- Obtains, clarifies, and verifies information through questioning

Personal Qualities/Work Ethic

- Displays self-esteem
- Knows self-management
- Takes responsibility
- Expresses willingness to learn
- Is motivated
- Understands need for organization, supervision, rules, policies and procedures

Interpersonal/Teamwork Skills

- Conducts self according to the expressed or unexpressed norms of a group and participates according to his or her talents
- Demonstrates respect for opinions, customs, and individual differences of others
- Handles conflict maturely
- Participates in group decisions
- Appreciates the importance and value of humor
- Offers and accepts criticism constructively

Soft skills differ from other skills in two related respects. First, the application of soft skills tends to be situation or environment specific, requiring an abili-

ty to discern what is appropriate in a particular environment. Hence, it is difficult
to evaluate them outside a context. Although some technical skills are environment specific, their appropriate applications in different situations can usually be
defined in advance. In contrast, the exercise of a soft skill does not involve a
sequence of actions that can be outlined and codified. The outcomes of any particular sequence of actions are likely to vary from one situation to the next.

A study of soft skills in the U.S. Army provides an excellent example, as
well as one of the earliest published uses of the phrase "soft skills." In a 1972
training manual, the Army defined soft skills as "job related skills involving
actions affecting primarily people and paper." In an effort to validate this definition, two researchers asked officers to categorize the skill "reading a map."
Reading a map clearly involves putting hand to paper, not using machines; however, most officers felt that reading a map was not a soft skill because it involved
a specific action with known consequences. In contrast, "motivating troops"
involves a more generalized action with uncertain consequences. While it is
quite possible to define *a priori* the precise steps required to read a map, it is
impossible to do so for motivating troops. Hence, reading a map is not really a
soft skill while motivating troops is.[11]

Of the skills listed in Table 5.1, practical cognition is likely to be the most
controversial. The critical distinction is between general intelligence as measured by standardized tests and common sense or "street smarts." Traditional
intelligence tests tend to measure the ability to perform tasks under conditions
disembodied from an individual's ordinary experience. The problems to be
solved are usually well defined, have one correct answer, and often only one
method of obtaining that correct answer. In contrast, practical cognition
involves solving poorly defined problems with incomplete information in con-
texts where there are likely to be multiple correct solutions.

The exercise of practical cognition, like other soft skills, tends to be context specific. What may be acceptable and indeed expected behavior in some
work environments can be unacceptable in others. The cultural norms of a construction site are quite different from those of an insurance office. While some
environments demand only standard English, in other environments a worker
who doesn't speak Spanish will be ineffective. Kevin Hollenbeck's 1994 study
of employers in Kalamazoo, Michigan, found broad agreement across industries
that soft skills were important, but wide variation in the relative importance
accorded different soft skills.[12] In a 1988 survey of employers of clerical workers

in California, Virginia Gaustad found that the soft skills required of clerk typists differed from those required of secretaries.[13]

In addition, the ability of any one worker to adapt to the norms of a workplace will depend on the behavior of other workers and supervisors. Again the military provides an example. Commenting on the problem of assessing the soft skills of army officers, Paul Whitmore has observed, "Whether or not a worker behaves in a 'motivated' fashion depends largely on how other people in his work environment treat him."[14] A black worker in a racially hostile environment may have difficulty functioning as a member of a team.

Because soft skills are invisible without a context, any assessment that takes place outside of a specific work environment will be incomplete. Nevertheless, a number of studies have used paper and pencil methods to assess soft skills. Several have used scores on standardized tests like the Armed Forces Qualification test to measure cognitive or problem-solving skills.[15] Greg Duncan and Rachel Dunifon relied on an index of motivation constructed from data in the Panel Survey of Income Dynamics to assess the impact of soft skills on long-term success in the labor market.[16] Some paper and pencil instruments to measure soft skills are being marketed by private consultants.

Soft skills fit the classic model of an experience good. An experience good is a good whose quality can be ascertained only through repeated use. Information about a worker's soft skills is necessarily incomplete until the worker has been hired and has been on the job for a period of time. When making the decision to hire a worker, employers will rely on indicators of soft skills such as past welfare receipt, characteristics of the worker's neighborhood, and school attended. These indicators may or may not reflect the abilities of the individual worker. Imperfect information also leads employers to rely on recruitment methods, such as employee referrals, that will pre-screen employees for the requisite soft skills.

Personal interviews represent another source of information about soft skills. The personal interview permits a direct assessment of the job candidate's communication skills and knowledge of appropriate dress and grooming. Interviewers rely on nonverbal cues to infer other attributes such as energy level and motivation.[17] Harry Holzer found that personal interviews were used to screen applicants for 87 percent of non-college jobs in central cities and suburbs.[18]

Because employers cannot observe soft skills prior to making a hiring decision, the added emphasis on these skills creates an environment conducive to statistical discrimination. Statistical discrimination occurs when an employer assesses the characteristics of an individual based on a stereotype about a group to which the individual belongs. For example, if the incidence of tardiness has been higher among single mothers than among childless women, employers may be more likely to hire the childless woman even if all the other characteristics of competing female applicants are identical.

Cultural differences may exacerbate this problem. Even if an employer knows that average skill levels are the same for two racial groups, he may be better able to judge the characteristics of his own group. If he is better able to identify the high-quality workers in his own group, he will be more likely to hire them than other equally qualified applicants.[19]

In addition, employers who exercise tastes for discrimination can easily cite "lack of soft skills" as a rationale for not hiring workers from specific neighborhoods or racial groups. Thus workers who apply for jobs from these neighborhoods or racial groups may suspect that lack of "soft skills" is really a euphemism for "wrong color," and this suspicion may reduce incentives to improve soft skills. This is complicated by the role of intermediaries — supervisors and other employees — whose attitudes and behavior will have an impact on a worker's ability to function in a specific environment. For example, if a supervisor uses a racial epithet or makes more subtle, coded references to race and the worker reacts negatively either through body language, facial expression or verbal challenge, the worker could be labeled as lacking soft skills.

DO AFRICAN AMERICAN WORKERS LACK SOFT SKILLS?

Given the discussion in the previous section, this paper may seem to have an impossible task. If soft skills are inherently context specific and not easily quantified, how do we assess the soft skills of African American workers? In existing studies of soft skills and race, the subjective judgements of employers are used to assess the soft skills of African American workers. These assessments are either obtained directly, through interviews, or indirectly, through observation of employer behavior. Employer assessment is an important source of information but, as noted above, it can be tainted by the racial prejudices of employers. One alternative is to focus on the subjective assessments of employers who might be less likely to harbor prejudices — employers who are members of racial minorities themselves.

Another source of information is direct assessment, using paper and pencil approaches or drawing inferences from worker behavior. For example, certain employee behaviors such as excessive absenteeism and tardiness might be indicative of poor work attitude or lack of other "soft skills."

Employer Assessments

In face-to-face interviews, urban employers frequently express negative opinions of the soft skills of black and Hispanic workers. In 1991 and 1992, Philip Moss and Chris Tilly conducted 66 interviews with 75 employer representatives at 55 organizations in Detroit and Los Angeles. Of those interviewed, 32 percent described black men as defensive, hostile, and having a difficult attitude, and 40 percent described black men as unmotivated employees.[20] Joleen Kirschenman and Kathryn Neckerman interviewed 185 employers in Cook County (including Chicago) in 1988 and 1989. When asked about differences in the work ethic of whites, blacks, and Hispanics, 38 percent of these employers ranked blacks last, and 7.6 percent of employers ranked blacks and Hispanics as sharing last place. A little more than one percent of employers ranked Hispanics last, but no employer ranked whites last. The remaining 51.4 percent either saw no difference or refused to categorize by race.[21]

Because these attitudes sound suspiciously like racist stereotypes, the authors of both studies emphasize in their findings that minority employers expressed similar opinions of the soft skills of black workers.[22] As a follow-up to its 1993 mail survey of minority-owned businesses, the Joint Center for Political and Economic Studies conducted face-to-face interviews with a small sample of minority-owned businesses in the Los Angeles area. This study found less unanimity than the others found in assessments of the soft skills of African American workers, and it found a general reluctance to identify soft skills as an obstacle to employment. For example, when queried about the soft skills of young black males relative to other workers, an Asian American owner of a janitorial services company commented that "young blacks have less exposure to the world of work and so may need more hand holding." An African American employer of truck drivers commented, "If a man has the skills I need, I'm willing to work with him. Suppose he uses street talk in his interview. I'll say,

'Listen, do you know how to talk a different way? Because when you talk to my customers you can't talk like that.'" Respondents identified characteristics other than race as indicators of soft skills. For example, one Latino marketing research executive expressed reluctance to hire former welfare recipients because "they think that if they show up for work they should get paid, regardless of what they do while they're here."[23]

Not all employers offered negative assessments. From interviews conducted in Atlanta, Georgia, Kirschenman (et al.) reported several examples of positive stereotypes of minority inner city workers. For example, one operations executive for a grocery chain commented, "In terms of work ethic I would tell you probably some of the inner city stores have a better work ethic than some of our northeast Atlanta stores."[24] Overall, less than half of employers in the surveys by Moss and Tilly and by Kirschenman gave negative assessments of the skills of black workers.

If employers believe that African Americans lack soft skills, then they should show less willingness to employ them in jobs where soft skills are more important relative to other jobs. Moss and Tilly used a multivariate analysis to explore the determinants of the racial composition of a firm's work force.[25] Employers who listed soft skills as the most important quality they sought in applicants did not hire a significantly smaller proportion of black workers than other employers did. Moss and Tilly also found that an employer's negative perceptions of the soft skills of black men had no effect on the racial composition of his work force.[26]

How does one explain the absence of a link between soft skills and minority employment in a multivariate analysis, given the prevalence of negative stereotypes among employers? Moss and Tilly argue that the problem is measurement error. The variable in question — whether employees mentioned soft skills first in describing 'desired employee qualities' — may not be a very accurate measure of the degree of importance employers attach to these skills. Yet even when Holzer used a different measure of skill requirements, he did not find a strong link between soft skill requirements and the racial composition of the work force.[27]

Another possibility is that whereas Moss and Tilly focused on race, employers are using class and neighborhood to judge the soft skills of workers. If employers base the judgement on neighborhood, then while the relationship between black employment and soft skills could be weak, the relationship between soft skills and the employment of black workers from specific neighborhoods could be quite strong. For example, an employer might give a high rating to the soft skills of black workers from a middle-class community but a low rating to workers from a low-income housing project. If the employer in this example considered soft skills important, he might hire the same proportion of black entry-level workers as other entry-level workers, while hiring significantly fewer residents from the housing project.[28] Moss and Tilly did not investigate whether such patterns occur.

Direct Assessment of Workers

Because soft skills are so difficult to assess, little direct evidence is available to corroborate or refute the negative stereotypes so many employers hold. Although recent studies link racial differences in labor market status to gaps in cognitive skills, it is not clear that the evidence provides any information on practical cognition. There are a few studies that examine the issues of work ethic, absenteeism, and tardiness.

George Farkas (et al.) argues that lower average cognitive skill levels of African American and Mexican American men "explain a substantial proportion of the earnings gap between these groups and European Americans." According to Farkas, racial and ethnic differences in cognitive skill lead to occupational sorting and to earnings differences within occupations. African Americans and Mexican Americans occupy jobs that require less cognitive skill than jobs held by European Americans with similar education and work experience and that pay lower wages. Within occupations, moreover, workers with lower levels of cognitive ability receive lower pay.[29] Holzer's findings corroborate these results. He found that the black males were less likely to be employed in jobs that require cognitive skills. Holzer did not find a similar limitation for black women, but Paula England (et al.) argues that differences in cognitive skills help explain differences in the occupational distributions of black, Latina, and Anglo women.[30]

A critical issue in these studies is whether the instrument used to measure cognitive skills is adequate to the task. Farkas (et al.) and England (et al.) both used the combined score on the Armed Forces Vocational Aptitude Battery of subtests of the Armed Forces Qualifications Test (AFQT). These are tests of word knowledge, paragraph comprehension, arithmetic reasoning, and math knowledge. Although performance on standardized tests like the AFQT correlates with job performance, it isn't clear that these tests measure either problem-solving ability or practical cognition.[31] Practical cognition and academic intelligence are not the same thing. Measures of academic intelligence show that it declines with age, whereas measures of problem solving ability and practical cognition tend to improve with age.[32] Not only do intelligence test scores imperfectly model problem-solving ability; they also may not measure the same thing for blacks and for whites. Critics of the tests argue that they are culturally biased because they actually measure people's exposure to the values of the white middle class. When test scores are adjusted for this cultural bias, these critics contend, their efficacy in explaining racial differences in earnings is reduced.[33]

Perhaps the most enduring criticism of black workers is that they lack a work ethic. Economists try to measure willingness to work by examining workers' reservation wages. The reservation wage is the lowest wage a worker would accept to leave unemployment for a job. In surveys, young black males name reservation wages similar to those named by whites when asked if they would accept a specific low-skilled job, such as dishwasher, at various hourly rates. However, when asked about the wages they would accept for jobs they were actually seeking, black men report reservation wages 11 to 13 percent higher than those reported by whites with similar qualifications.[34] Some observers interpret this finding as confirmation that young blacks are not interested in working for a living,[35] while others regard it as evidence that blacks are unwilling to lower their reservation wages to accommodate labor market discrimination.[36]

Stephen Pettersen disputes both these interpretations, arguing that the ratio of the reservation wage to predicted or past wage is a poor predictor of willingness to work. Reservation wages, according to Pettersen, reflect aspirations and perceptions of self worth and do not determine what the jobless do when they are actually offered a job. Furthermore, using data from the National Longitudinal Survey of Youth, a multi-year survey sponsored by the Bureau of Labor Statistics focusing on the labor market experiences of American men and women,[37] Pettersen found that white and black youth have similar reservation wages when past wage is held constant.[38]

Absenteeism and tardiness provide alternative indicators of willingness to work. Data from the U.S. Census Bureau's Current Population Survey indicate that black youths are absent from work more often than white youths.[39] In a study of postal workers, however, Craig Zwerling and Hilary Silver found that black postal workers were less likely to be absent from their jobs than were their white counterparts.[40] Some of the racial differences in absenteeism may reflect differences in job characteristics. Absenteeism is higher in jobs that are unpleasant, and black workers occupy a disproportionate share of such jobs. Studies of the determinants of tardiness produce similar results — tardiness is correlated with characteristics other than race of the worker. Years of work experience and marriage reduce the incidence of tardiness, while holding a high-paying job[41] and working excessive overtime increase tardiness. When researchers control statistically for these factors, race turns out not to play a significant role.[42]

HOW DOES A WORKER ACQUIRE SOFT SKILLS?

Even if African American workers do not lack soft skills relative to other workers, the problem for the individual remains the same. If he possesses the required soft skills, he must persuade employers that he has them. If he doesn't possess them, he must acquire them and then persuade the employer that he has them. Hence, a critical component of any soft skills training must be establishing credibility with employers. A program that successfully develops an individual's soft skills could still fail to have an impact on employment if employers did not recognize the program's value.

Soft skills training for entry-level workers achieved notoriety in 1998 with the airing of a *60 Minutes* segment on the STRIVE program in New York City.[43] The news story described STRIVE's (Support and Training Results in Valuable Employment) three-week boot-camp style training course, which emphasizes communications skills and personal qualities such as dress, attitude, and punctuality. Although the STRIVE program is being imitated across the country, not all private training programs follow this model.

The Joint Center for Political and Economic Studies' compilation of 54 programs that offer soft skills training reveals rich variety.[44] The majority (76 percent) of the programs surveyed, like STRIVE, rely on classroom instruction. At STRIVE, participants attend workshops, sessions, and technology lessons each day from 9:00 a.m. to 5:00 p.m. The Work Connections Center in West Plains, Missouri, also relies on classroom based instruction, but in its four-to-six-week course the classroom is set up to simulate a work environment. Instructors represent employers, and supervisors and participants stand in as employees. Participants are expected to abide by rules similar to the workplace — punctuality and proper dress and decorum. Other programs combine classroom training with experiential learning through internships and work assignments. For example, the YouthBuild program in Rockford, Illinois, trains young people for construction industry jobs. Participants engage in classroom activities two days a week, work two days a week on a construction site, and fulfill community service requirements on Fridays. The Factory Program, operated by the Lester and Rosalie Anixter Center in Chicago, divides each day of training into halves, devoting the first part to individualized academic instruction and the second part to vocational education and hands-on skills training.

Most of the programs combine soft skills training with either basic academic preparation (study for the GED) or technical skills training. Only 24 percent of the programs focus solely on soft skills. For example, the STRIVE-NY program offers training in word processing and typing. The Industrial Exchange (IndEx), based in Tulsa, Oklahoma, provides vocational training in light manufacturing, assembly packaging, telecommunications, data entry, basic electronics, pneumatics, hydraulics, measurements, customer service, and computer use. A small percentage of the training programs focus on preparing applicants for a specific occupation or industry. For example, Home Care Associates of Philadelphia trains low-income individuals as Certified Nurse Assistants and Certified Medicare Home Health Aides.

Almost all of the programs surveyed by the Joint Center offer follow-up services to their clients. Most offer these services for at least a month. Some offer them indefinitely. In most cases, graduates can return to the programs for additional training, for job placement assistance, or to participate in support groups. Few of the programs link the follow-up services to the job placement. An exception is Home Care Associates of Philadelphia, where a job coach collects feedback from supervisors, coworkers, and customers and meets with the worker and her supervisors to resolve any problems that arise. Hence, the training happens in the context of a specific work environment.

Programs reported high levels of success in job placement and retention. Placement and retention rates[45] reported to the Joint Center ranged from 50 percent for the Chicago Commons West Humboldt Employment Training Center and the Factory Program (also in Chicago), to more than 80 percent among graduates of the STRIVE program's East Harlem Employment Service and the Adult Career Educational Services program at the Curtis Park Community Center in Denver. However, these are raw numbers that do not account for the differing characteristics of program participants. Without examining the percentages while controlling for differences, we cannot know whether many of the graduates would have found employment without attending the programs. Also, because many of these programs combined soft skills training with other training, the high job placement and retention rates could just as easily reflect the effectiveness of the training in academic and technical skills.

Moreover, a program can have high placement and retention rates not because it teaches soft skills, but because it screens out workers who lack them. The boot camp atmosphere of a program like STRIVE comes at a high cost for the participants. The STRIVE program dictated participants' dress, speech, and even facial expressions; those who were unable or unwilling to adapt to this left the program. Success in STRIVE did effectively measure a person's ability to follow rules and regulations and to adapt to a cultural norm. Thanks in part to the publicity generated by *60 Minutes*, potential employers appreciated the fact that attrition from the program says something good about those who graduate from it.[46]

Another approach to establishing credibility with employers is to have employers participate directly in the training process either by locating the training at the workplace or by inviting employers to teach or direct the training at a training facility. Intuitively, workplace or apprenticeship learning offers two advantages over classroom instruction. First, trainees must abide by the fuzzy rules and social norms of a specific workplace rather than by the artificially well-defined rules of a training program. Second, employers have the opportunity to observe an individual's soft skills first-hand before making a commitment to long-term employment. Prior knowledge of the individual should make the employer less likely to engage in statistical discrimination.

Given these potential advantages, it is surprising that only a few of the programs surveyed by the Joint Center incorporate experiential learning. The school-to-work initiative held some promise in this regard. Although the initiative was not explicitly a soft skills training program, it linked classroom-based education with experiential learning through internships, mentor programs, and jobs. It had three components: school-based activities, work-based activities, and connecting activities. School-based activities involve classroom instruction that is linked to workplace experience and may include interest inventories, visits to businesses and job sites, and individualized career plans. Work-based activities included paid work experience, job shadowing, internships, and apprenticeships. Connecting activities included internships for teachers and participation in school-to-work conferences. The School-to-Work Opportunities Act expired in October 2001 and was not renewed. A national evaluation of school-to-work programs conducted by Mathematica Policy Research found a diverse mix of student participants in school-to-work programs. Sixty-three percent of all students participated in comprehensive career development programs, 16 percent in workplace activity linked to school, and 12 percent in career related academic programs. African American students, particularly females, had a higher propensity to participate in cooperative education activities — that is, jobs that were linked with a school class and counted toward its grade.[47]

The impact of school-to-work on participants' soft skills is largely speculative at this point. However, future researchers may be able to utilize the NLSY data to study labor market impacts, since the 1998 NLSY survey included questions on participation in school-to-work programs.

Although this discussion has concentrated on training for entry-level or low-skill workers, soft skills are also a requirement for professional and managerial jobs. Indeed, my own survey of the extant journal articles uncovered far more references to the soft skills required of computer programmers than to those required of hotel bellhops.[48] Training techniques for management and professional workers vary from computer-assisted to mentoring programs, but the issues that emerge in the literature are remarkably similar to the ones raised here.[49] James Georges argues that it is difficult to show concrete results from soft skills courses because they are a form of education (which increases intellectual awareness of a subject) rather than a form of training (which makes someone proficient at the execution of a given task).[50] Marie Strebler argues that the subjectivity inherent in the assessment of soft skills explains the lack of advancement of women in management despite the stereotype that women are better at interpersonal relations.[51]

In the absence of objective tools to assess workers' soft skills, rigorous evaluations of the impact of relevant training programs may not be possible. Nevertheless, an analysis of current programs does suggest two general principles. One, soft skills training and training in the more technical aspects of a job are complements, not substitutes. Most programs offer both types of training. Furthermore, although a smile may increase the likelihood that a worker is hired, its marginal effect is likely to be greater if the worker also has computer skills.

Two, training programs must do more than teach a worker soft skills; they must also address the problem of "imperfect information." Imperfect information refers to the fact that employers cannot observe a worker's soft skills before hiring him. Thus, an employer who hires a new worker incurs a risk that the worker will lack soft skills. The situation is similar to that faced by a consumer who wants to try a new brand of shampoo or a used car. The consumer cannot assess the effect of the shampoo on his hair without trying it. He cannot completely assess the quality of the new car until he has driven for a few weeks. Because of imperfect information, consumers tend to rely on guarantees, brand names (in the case of shampoo), or independent certifications such as provided by trusted car repairman (in the case of a car). One strategy to increase an employer's willingness to hire a worker who's soft skills are in doubt is to offer guarantees,[52] independent certification (such as a credible testing instrument), or even the development of brand names.[53]

IMPLICATIONS FOR PUBLIC POLICY

A major question for public policy is whether the private market will produce optimal investment in soft skills training. Economic theory predicts that workers will invest in their general skills — skills that retain their value from one employer to the next — and that firms will invest in firm-specific skills — skills that lose their value once a worker leaves his current employer. In theory, with no liquidity constraints, private decision-makers in perfectly competitive markets will invest in the optimal level of job training, and no government intervention is needed. Even with liquidity constraints, a worker can pay for training in general skills by accepting a wage lower than his marginal product for a fixed training period.[54]

Soft skills complicate this theoretical scenario in two ways. First, soft skills do not easily fit the firm-specific vs. general skill dichotomy. Second, there is the problem of imperfect information. These problems lead to an under-investment in soft skills even when workers face no constraints on liquidity.

Some soft skills clearly represent general human capital. The ability to communicate clearly in English is transferable from one employer to another. Other soft skills, most notably teamwork, are a hybrid of general and firm-specific skills. Although some component of teamwork ability is likely to be transferable from one team to another, other components are team-specific — and hence, workplace-specific. Practical cognition is another hybrid, neither completely general nor purely specific. Even though the exercise of soft skills may be context-specific, the underlying ability to decode an environment — to recognize the modes of behavior appropriate to an employment context — retains its value from one employer to the next.

An employer has an incentive to invest in the improvement of hybrid skills if he will benefit from the increase in productivity without an offsetting increase in worker's wages. In the National Center on the Education Quality of the Workforce's National Employer Survey, a collaborative effort of the Institute for Research on Higher Education and the Wharton School at the University of Pennsylvania, 54 percent of establishments engage in teamwork or problem-solving training.[55] Yet, employers are likely to invest less in hybrid skills training than is socially optimal, because the positive externalities — the spillover benefits to workers and to future employers — will not enter their calculations. The worker, on the other hand, will also invest too little because his paycheck will not fully reflect the increase in his value to the firm.

Imperfect assessment information also affects the worker's investment decision. Because a firm cannot perfectly assess a worker's soft skills, a worker may not be able to recoup the full value of training. An investment in the development of soft skills is thus riskier than investments in more technical skills or in more traditional academic skills. The problem may be especially acute for minority workers. If differences in culture or stereotypes affect an employer's assessment of soft skills, minority workers may have greater difficulty recouping their investment.

Without government intervention, there is likely to be too little investment in soft skill development. Hence, there is clearly a rationale for public subsidy. However, in the case of soft skills, the public sector has a role beyond the provision of dollars for training. Information imperfections create a role for government as an evaluator of training practices, as a source of independent certification, and as an information provider. In addition, information imperfections complicate the government's role as enforcer of equal employment opportunity laws. An employer who fails to hire a black job applicant may argue that the applicant lacks soft skills. The problem for public policy is to evaluate the legitimacy of such a claim. A resolution to this problem is important, because if enforcers of anti-discrimination laws fail to detect false claims of soft skill deficits, this would in turn undermine the credibility of soft skills training with the workers and reduce their incentives to participate.

CONCLUSIONS

A significant minority of employers believes that African American workers lack soft skills relative to other groups, and not all of these employers are white. These opinions cannot be readily corroborated with facts nor can they be glibly attributed to discrimination. Even if employers perceive a deficit where one doesn't exist, this still poses an obstacle to employment that must be addressed.

In other words, soft skills do seem to matter. In national inventories of the skills needed for employment, in surveys of employers in specific industries and occupations, and in surveys of employers of entry-level workers, employers consistently list communication skills, interpersonal skills, and problem-solving skills as critical to workforce productivity. They appear to pay a wage premium to workers who possess soft skills — to workers with high self esteem,[56] to workers with higher levels of cognitive ability, as measured on standardized tests,[57] and to workers with higher indices of motivation.[58]

The difficult question is exactly how *much* soft skills matter. Answering that question will require a fuller assessment of the soft skills deficits of African American and other entry-level workers; an evaluation of training programs to identify best practices; and finally, a mechanism to provide credible information to employers about applicants' soft skills.

NOTES

1. Philip Moss and Chris Tilly, "Soft Skills and Race: An Investigation of Black Men's Employment Problems." *Work and Occupations* 23 (August 1995): 252-276; and "Skills and Race in Hiring: Quantitative Findings From Face-To-Face Interviews," *Eastern Economic Journal* (Summer 1996): 357-374; William Julius Wilson, *When Work Disappears: The World of the New Urban Poor* (New York: Alfred A. Knopf, 1997); Joleen Kirschenman and Kathryn M. Neckerman, "'We'd Love to Hire Them, But...' The Meaning of Race for Employers" in *The Urban Underclass*, edited by Christopher Jencks and Paul E. Peterson (Washington, D.C.: The Brookings Institution, 1991); Joleen Kirschenman, Philip Moss, and Chris Tilly, *Employer Screening Methods and Racial Exclusion: Evidence from New In-Depth Interviews with Employers* (New York: Russell Sage Foundation 1995).

2. Moss and Tilly, "Skills and Race in Hiring"; Harry Holzer, *What Employers Want: Job Prospects for Less-Educated Workers* (New York: Russell Sage Foundation, 1996) and "Barriers to Higher Employment Rates Among African Americans," in *Job Creation: Prospects and Strategies*, edited by Wilhelmina A. Leigh and Margaret C. Simms (Washington DC: Joint Center for Political and Economic Studies, 1998); Kevin Hollenbeck, "The Workplace Know-How Skills Needed to Be Productive" (Technical Report prepared by The Upjohn Institute for Kalamazoo County Education for Employment Outcomes Task Force, May 1994).

3. Cecilia Conrad, *Soft Skills: A Guide to Informed Discussion* (Washington, DC: Joint Center for Political and Economic Studies, 1999).

4. Rosemary Cafasso, "Selling Your Soft Side (People Skills Win You the Job)," *Computerworld* 30 (1 April, 1996): 97; Dwight B. Davis, "Hard Demand for Soft Skills," *Datamation* 39 (15 January 1993): 28-32.; Melanie Menagh, "Made to Order," *Computerworld* 30 (19 August, 1996): 78.

5. Lori Bongiorno, "Ivy and Innovation: B-Schools Try Harder," *Business Week* (7 June, 1993): 114-15.

6. See DeVry's web site at www.devry.edu.

7. SCANS 1992. The work of the SCANS commission has been continued under the auspices of the National Skills Standards Board (NSSB), http://www.nssb.org/. The NSSB is orchestrating voluntary programs within industry sectors to define skill standards and the develop common assessment tools and certification methods.

8. Harold F. O'Neil, Keith Alfred, and Eva L. Baker, "Measurement of Workforce Readiness: Review of Theoretical Frameworks," Research Paper (National Center for Research on Evaluation, Standards and Student Testing, ERIC Document ED353328, 1993).

9. Anthony Patrick Carnevale, *America and the New Economy* (The American Society for Training and Development and the U.S. Department of Labor, Employment, and Training Administration, 1991).

10. Moss and Tilly, "Skills and Race in Hiring."

11. John P. Fry and Paul G. Whitmore, "What Are Soft Skills?" Papers presented at the CONARC Soft Skills Conference, Fort Bliss, Texas, December 1972.

12. Hollenbeck, "The Workplace Know-How Skills Needed to Be Productive."

13. Virginia M. Gaustad, "Qualities and Skills Employers Like and Dislike in Clerical Workers: An Office Administration Survey" (San Bernadino Community College District, Office of Planning and Research, 1988).

14. Paul G. Whitmore, "The Behavioral Model as a Tool for Analyzing Soft Skills." Paper presented at CONARC Soft Skills Conference, Fort Bliss, Texas, December 1972.

15. George Farkas, Paula England, Keven Vicknair, and Barbara Stanek Kilbourne, "Cognitive Skill, Skill Demands of Jobs, and Earnings Among Young European American, African American, and Mexican American Workers," *Social Forces* 75 (March 1997): 913-940.; June O'Neil, "The Role of Human Capital in Earnings Differences Between Black and White Men," *The Journal of Economic Perspectives* 4 (Fall, 1990): 25-46.

16. Greg J. Duncan and Rachel Dunifon, "Soft-Skills and Long-Run Labor Market Success," *Research in Labor Economics* 17, 1998: pp 123-149.

17. Robert Gifford, Cheuk Fan Ng, and Margaret Wilkinson, "Nonverbal Cues in the Employment Interview: Links Between Applicant Qualities and Interviewer Judgements," *Journal of Applied Psychology* 70 (No. 4): 729-736; Charles K. Parsons and Robert C. Liden, "Interviewer Perceptions of Applicant Qualifications: A Multivariate Field Study of Demographic Characteristics and Nonverbal Cues," *Journal of Applied Psychology* 69 (No.4): 557-568.

18. Harry Holzer, *What Employers Want: Job Prospects for Less-Educated Workers* (New York: Russell Sage Foundation 1996).

19. Bradford Cornell and Ivo Welch, "Culture, Information, and Screening Discrimination," *Journal of Political Economy*, Vol. 104, pp. 542-571.

20. Moss and Tilly, "Skills and Race in Hiring"; Holzer, *What Employers Want* and "Barriers to Higher Employment Rates Among African Americans."

21. Kirschenman and Neckerman, "We'd Love to Hire Them, But…"

22. William Julius Wilson, *When Work Disappears: The World of the New Urban Poor* (New York: Alfred A. Knopf, 1997).

23. Personal interview conducted by the author with business owner, July 1999.

24. Kirschenman, et al., "Employer Screening Methods and Racial Exclusion."

25. Moss and Tilly, "Soft Skills and Race."

26. Moss and Tilly, "Soft Skills and Race."

27. Holzer, *What Employers Want.*

28. Moss and Tilly study only entry-level jobs and workers.

29. Farkas et al., "Cognitive Skill, Skill Demands of Jobs, and Earnings Among Young European American, African American, and Mexican American Workers"; June O'Neil, "The Role of Human Capital in Earnings Differences Between Black and White Men," *The Journal of Economic Perspectives* 4 (Fall, 1990): 25-46.

30. Paula England, Karen Christopher, and Lori L. Reid, "Gender, Race, Ethnicity, and Wages," in *Latinas and African American Women at Work: Race, Gender and Economic Inequality*, edited by Irene Brown (New York: Russell Sage Foundation, 1999).

31. Farkas et al., "Cognitive Skill, Skill Demands of Jobs, and Earnings Among Young European American, African American, and Mexican American Workers"; O'Neil, "The Role of Human Capital in Earnings Differences Between Black and White Men"; and England et al., "Gender, Race, Ethnicity, and Wages."

32. Robert J. Sternberg, Richard K. Wagner, Wendy M. Williams, and Joseph A. Horvath, "Practical Cognition" (http://nces.ed.gov/ilss/documents/practcog.pdf. Accessed June, 2000).

33. William M. Rodgers III and William E. Spriggs, "What Does the AFQT Really Measure: Race, Wages, Schooling and the AFQT Score," *Review of Black Political Economy* 24 (Spring): 13-46; David J. Maume Jr., A. Silvia Cancio, and T. David Evans, "Cognitive Skills and Racial Wage Inequality: Reply to Farkas and Vicknair," *American Sociological Review* 61 (August): 561-564.

34. Holzer, *What Employers Want.*

35. Lawrence M. Mead, *The New Politics of Poverty: The Nonworking Poor in America.* (New York: Basic Books, 1992).

36. Holzer, *What Employers Want.*

37. For more information on the National Longitudinal Surveys, the reader is referred to http://www.chrr.ohio-state.edu/nls-info/surveys.php3.

38. Stephen Pettersen, "Are Young Black Men Really Less Willing to Work?" *American Sociological Review* 62 (August): 605-661.

39. Ron Ferguson and Randall Filer, "Do Better Jobs Make Better Workers? Absenteeism from Work Among Inner-City Black Youths," In *The Black Youth Employment Crisis*, edited by Richard B. Freemand and Harry Holzer (Chicago: University of Chicago Press, 1986).

40. Craig Zwerling and Hilary Silver, "Race and Job Dismissals in a Federal Bureaucracy," *American Sociological Review* 57 (October 1992): 651-660.

41. This result may seem puzzling at first. One possible explanation is that in high paying jobs give the worker more flexibility and relief from direct supervision, thus the worker essentially sets his own hours.

42. J.Paul Leigh and John Lust, "Punctuality and Tardiness in Supplying Labor," *Atlantic Economic Journal* 14 (July, 1986): 6-25; and "Determinants of Employee Tardiness," *Work and Occupations* 15 (February, 1998): 78-95.

43. *60 Minutes* aired a follow-up story on October 17, 1999.

44. Wilhelmina A. Leigh, Deitra H. Lee, and Malinda A. Lindquist, *Soft Skills Training: An Annotated Guide to Selected Programs* (Washington, DC: Joint Center for Political and Economic Studies, 1999).

45. Some programs reported retention rates – what percentage of workers were still holding jobs a specified number of weeks or months after training ended. Other programs reported placement rates – what percentage of workers were placed in jobs after training ended.

46. STRIVE had a reputation for high attrition rates, but no specific data was available on actual attrition.

47. Alan M. Hershey, Marsha K. Silverberg, Joshua Harrison, Paula Hudis, and Russell Jackson, *Expanding Options For Students: Report to Congress on the National Evaluation of School-to-Work Implementation* (Princeton, N.J.: Mathematica Policy Research, February,1999).

48. Conrad, *Soft Skills.*

49. Dena J. Heathman and Brian H. Kleiner, "Training and Technology: The Future is Now," *Training and Development* 45 (September): 49-51; Allison Rosset and Jeremy Barnett,

"Designing Under the Influence (Need for Instructional Design Using Multimedia Systems)," *Training* 33 (December): 34-7; Linda Wilson, "Yearn to Learn," *Computerworld* (June): 41-3.

50. James C. Georges, "The Myth of Soft Skills Training," *Training* 33 (January): 48-50.

51. Marie Strebler, "Soft Skills and Hard Questions," *People Management* 3 (29 May): 20-4.

52. Sandhill Community College in Pinehurst, North Carolina, provides a guarantee to employers that graduates will be proficient and work ready. If the employer is dissatisfied, the employee can re-enroll in courses at no cost to the employee or the employer.

53. The reputation of a school or training program can function like a brand name.

54. An excellent summary of these results is found in K. Deron Acemoglu and Steve Pischke, "Why Do Firms Train? Theory and Evidence," *Quarterly Journal of Economics* 113 (February 1998): 79-119.

55. Lisa M. Lynch and Sandra E. Black, *Beyond the Incidence of Training: Evidence from the National Employer Survey*, EQW Working Papers WP35 (Philadelphia: University of Pennsylvania, 1996).

56. Arthur H. Goldsmith, Jonathan R. Veum, and William A. Darity, Jr., "The Impact of Psychological and Human Capital and Wages," *Economic Inquiry* 35 (October): 815-829.

57. Farkas et al., "Cognitive Skill, Skill Demands of Jobs, and Earnings Among Young European American, African American, and Mexican American Workers."

58. Duncan and Dunifon, "Soft-Skills and Long-Run Labor Market Success."

Chapter Six

THE ROLE OF PUBLIC POLICY
IN SKILLS DEVELOPMENT
OF BLACK WORKERS
IN THE 21ST CENTURY

Timothy Bartik
Kevin Hollenbeck

INTRODUCTION

The current system for skills development in the United States is a combination of public and private education and training institutions. The "first chance" or conventional system allows individuals to proceed through an extensive public elementary, secondary, and postsecondary educational sector that is supplemented by private educational institutions and is followed by employer-provided job training and work experience. People invest time and effort in their schooling opportunities and gain general knowledge and skills that allow them to pursue jobs and careers. Once they have entered a career, they learn specific skills via job training and work experience. Of course, career pathways are not always linear; people may stop and restart their education and change jobs and careers as their personal interests and opportunities change.

The "second chance" system is designed for those who do not successfully traverse the first chance system. The second chance system is almost exclusively funded and administered by public agencies, although religious and other non-profit agencies are also active in the system. Public job training programs, public assistance, rehabilitation programs for offenders, and educational remedia-

Timothy Bartik and Kevin Hollenbeck are senior economists at the W.E. Upjohn Institute.

tion are important conduits of skill and talent development. The public agency for labor market exchange, the Employment Service, has also tended to play a significant role in facilitating employment in the second chance system.

The tremendous success of the U.S. economy, with the world's highest level of worker productivity, might lead us to assume that the skills development system in this country is a success. However, there is a pervasive perception that the current system is failing and that it is failing especially in urban areas where African Americans are concentrated. Lagging school achievement (particularly in urban areas), high unemployment rates for certain groups of the population, and employer concerns about the quality of entry-level workers suggest that our current system may be neither efficient nor equitable. Because of these concerns, a reexamination of the role of public policy in skills development seems appropriate.

In the next sections of the paper, we discuss governmental policy initiatives in both the first and second chance systems and ongoing or recent policy experimentation. We summarize the characteristics of education and training opportunities that seem to work, and we draw conclusions and implications about the potential effectiveness of the 1998 Workforce Investment Act (WIA).

Federal, State, and Local Policy Initiatives in the First Chance System

Federal involvement in the first chance system of skills development has been very limited over the years. Public education, particularly in the K-12 system, is viewed as a state responsibility, and on-the-job training is generally seen as an activity that should be paid for by those who benefit from it — employers and workers. Federal public policy has historically played a passive role — financing the provision of public elementary and secondary education and subsidizing post-secondary education. These social investments are justified economically on the grounds of spillover benefits.[1]

Over the last few decades, however, the government has intervened more actively in the regulation of educational processes because of concerns about equity of outcomes and access. Substantial resources and concomitant regulations targeted at special education and disadvantaged students have been developed as federal policymakers observed that children who had handicapping conditions or were economically disadvantaged tended to fare more poorly, on average, in elementary and secondary schools. Furthermore, as the cost of postsecondary education increased, the government actively provided funding in the form of grants and loans, recognizing that the private lending market is not set up to make loans available for investment in "human capital."

The federal government has funded technical (vocational) training in the public educational system since the Smith-Hughes Act was passed in 1917. The 1990 Perkins Act shifted the focus of these programs from training for specific occupations toward a broader preparation that integrates academic and vocational education. It encouraged collaboration between the secondary and post-secondary (particularly two-year) educational institutions through Tech-Prep programs. The 1998 Perkins Act (Perkins II) continues funding for these programs, but it also requires that states establish performance goals and regularly report their progress toward achieving them.

In 1994, Congress passed the School-to-Work Opportunities Act. This initiative provided seed money to states and local partnerships of business, labor, government, education, and community organizations to develop programs that stimulate the career development of young people. Its purpose was to integrate academic and workplace education for all students, not just those in vocational programs. School to Work programs comprised school-based activities, work-based learning, and activities meant to connect these two areas of instruction.

The Perkins Act and the School-to-Work Opportunities Act are particularly effective at preparing individuals for the sub-baccalaureate labor market — occupations requiring less than a four-year degree.[2] Official forecasts from the Department of Labor project significant growth in occupations such as technicians, programmers, medical aides, and craftspersons. Advocates for African Americans and other minorities should make sure that these groups have both reliable information about the potential payoff of sub-baccalaureate occupations and access to high-quality school-to-work or tech prep programs that prepare students for these careers.

Most recently, policy makers have begun bringing new regulation and government-sponsored programs into education, due to their concern about lagging student achievement. Goals 2000, enacted in 1994, supported development and implementation of state standards for student learning and achievement.

This thrust in federal policy reinforces actions at the state and local level. Two trends that are greatly influencing the delivery of instruction in K-12 education are the setting of curriculum standards at the state level and the institution of market-based approaches to educational reform. Currently 49 states (all

but Iowa) have established curriculum standards for public elementary and secondary systems. These standards are generally phrased as statements about what
students need to know about a subject and when they need to know it. The creation of these standards attests to the extent to which education now focuses on
student outcomes. Most states have instituted state-level standardized tests to
assess student learning. Many states (perhaps led by Texas and New York) have
adopted a "high-stakes" approach in which students are required to pass state
tests in order to receive a diploma or pass into the next grade.

Market-based approaches to educational reform include charter schools and
voucher/tax credits. Thirty-seven states have charter school legislation in which
individuals receive public support for establishing schools that offer alternatives to
traditional public schools. The underlying vision motivating the charter school
movement is that these schools will, to some extent, be laboratories to test innovative curriculum approaches; at the same time, public schools will be forced to
improve in response to the competition offered by the charter schools. With
voucher/tax credit programs, states provide eligible students with vouchers that can
be used for tuition payment at private schools, or they give students state income
tax credits for tuition or other education expenses. A voucher program that has
been operating in Milwaukee for a number of years has received a lot of research
attention;[3] the results to date suggest that students who use a voucher to attend
a private school show only slight improvement in achievement, but that parental
satisfaction with the voucher program is substantial.

Individuals concerned about the future labor market prospects of African
American youth should closely monitor the outcomes of both the standards
movement and the charter school/voucher approaches. Considerable evidence
shows that African Americans lag behind whites in standardized testing at
school-entry ages and that the gap has not closed by the time they graduate from
high school.[4] In the 1998 publication, *The Black-White Test Score Gap*, edited
by Christopher Jencks and Meredith Phillips, the authors offer a number of
hypotheses about why the formal education system fails to close the gap, but we
are particularly convinced by Ronald Ferguson's argument in that book that
holding lower expectations for lower-achieving students does great harm and
perpetuates the gap.[5] Empirical data suggest that teachers may hold lower expectations of their African American students and, therefore, not push them to reach
the same achievement levels as non-minority students. Tough, fair standards
imposed by states and backed up by assessment programs may result in raising

expectations for lower-achieving students so that they become more nearly equal, or even higher, than those for white students. On the other hand, if it is testing bias that is causing the gap in test scores of minorities,[6] then high-stakes tests may differentially penalize African Americans.

If the promise of charter schools as innovative alternatives to public schools is realized, then African Americans may be favorably impacted because urban areas are most likely to have the scale and enrollment to support charter schools. On the other hand, if charter schools turn out to be failures, then African Americans will be hurt disproportionately.[7]

Charter schools and vouchers are holistic reforms of education. A less expansive reform, but one that has direct implications for the skills development of students, is the renaissance in career and technical education. Until recently, career and technical education in secondary schooling was saddled with reputational baggage — historically, the vocational track was the "dumping ground" for students considered incorrigible or perceived to lack intellectual ability. But today, curriculum reform has moved toward an approach that views education as integrating career development and academic skills. Furthermore, the hands-on, project-based pedagogy of vocational education has been shown to match the learning styles of the majority of students.[8] Finally, shortages of skilled workers in the sub-baccalaureate labor market have become more and more a concern of employers, who are actively collaborating in the career and technical education system. Employer involvement in urban areas has been slow to develop, however, which may adversely affect black workers.

Federal, State, and Local Policy Initiatives in the Second Chance System

As noted above, the second chance system for skills development is almost entirely a public enterprise. The public sector assumes the financial burden for two reasons. The first reason is financial, and the second reason is "informational." If participants in the second chance system had to finance their own (re)training, they would likely find it very difficult to access the funds. Lenders would not be forthcoming because of the risk. These individuals did not succeed in the first chance system because they had learning obstacles that were not addressed, or they failed because the schools in the first chance system that they attended were inadequate — or both. Success in the second chance system is thus uncertain.

Furthermore, the benefit of succeeding in terms of increased wages or earnings may be modest. This problem is overcome by the government providing the training and assuming the risk.

Even when people successfully receive skills training in the second chance system, they may not be able to get a good job or progress in a career if they cannot signal their new skills. Economists refer to this problem as an informational deficiency. Once an individual has entered the labor force and begun a gainful career, upward progression or career changes usually rely on job or occupational changes. But often, employers are reluctant to hire individuals with irregular work histories or formal educational credentials. In these cases, there may be a need to develop public policies to certify skill competencies or otherwise facilitate the career progression of participants in the second chance system.

Federal job training programs. A number of federal programs are aimed at skills development of at-risk individuals. The federal government funds and administers direct job-training programs for a number of different populations in addition to the public labor market exchange; most recently, public assistance programs also emphasize skill development for individuals to use in the labor market.

The history of public job-training policy in the U.S. over the last few decades is punctuated by frequent change, and one of the most significant changes has been an evolution from centralization to decentralization. Table 6.1 provides a chronology of federal skills development programs. The Manpower Development and Training Act (MDTA) of 1962 was the first major federal job training program. Administered centrally by the U.S. Department of Labor, it was intended to provide training for workers who had been displaced by automation; for poorly educated, unskilled youth; and for adults who had been displaced and would have poor job prospects without additional training. Early in its implementation, MDTA shifted its emphasis away from workers displaced by automation toward severely disadvantaged workers.

It is clear from the historical evidence that minorities and women made substantial labor market gains in the 1960s. Eli Ginzberg suggests that some of the gains could be attributed to MDTA;[9] however, there were also two other important factors — the passing of civil rights legislation in 1964 and an expansionary economy and tight labor market in the latter half of the decade.

The MDTA lasted about 10 years and was succeeded by the Comprehensive Employment and Training Act (CETA) of 1973. CETA decentralized the admin-

TABLE 6.1: FEDERAL SKILLS DEVELOPMENT INITIATIVES

Vocational and Career Preparation

Program	Dates	Key Features
The 1990 Perkins Act (Perkins Tech-Prep)	1990-1998	Emphasis on integration of academic and vocational training; funded tech-prep programs, which were collaborative efforts between secondary and postsecondary educational institutions
School-to-Work	1994 - 2001	Advocates integration of academic and place education for all students, not just vocational students; supports classroom-based career preparation and work-based learning experiences
The 1998 Perkins Act (Perkins III)	1998 -	Strengthens requirements for performance measurement

Worker Training

Program	Dates	Key Features
Manpower Development and Training Act (MDTA)	1962-1972	Funded training for unemployed through vocational education institutions and the Employment Service
Comprehensive Employment Training Act (CETA)	1973-1982	Added public service component to and training;decentralized administration of public training program
Job Training Partnership Act (JTPA)	1983-2000	No public service employment; control of training in hands of private industry councils
Workforce Investment Act (WIA)	1998 -	Combines Employment Service with job training programs under direction of private-sector-led boards; introduces vouchers to finance education and training

istration of public training and provided funding directly to local governments. In addition, CETA added a public service employment component. With local discretion in the selection of training providers, CETA training tended to be provided by vocational education and community-based organizations. But the labor market gains by minorities were retrenched in the 1970s, largely because of a major recession in the early part of the decade followed by a stagflationary economy in the latter part. CETA was politically undone by media attention focused on bureaucratic, fraudulent, or politically motivated patronage practices in a few areas. First, the public service employment title was discontinued, and then the training titles followed. Ginzberg opines that the media attention, although not groundless, was overblown;[10] however, CETA program defenders had relatively few success stories, and those were mainly concentrated among lengthy training programs in particular sectors — automobile services and health care, for example.

In 1983, the Job Training Partnership Act (JTPA) was passed and implemented. JTPA was the major framework of federal job training policy until about 2000. It attempted to overcome public mistrust by having no public service employment and no training stipends, and by placing control in the hands of private industry councils (PICs) that were headed and numerically dominated by individuals from the private sector. Its major training programs were targeted on disadvantaged youth and adults and displaced workers.

In 1998, Congress passed the Workforce Investment Act (WIA), a major reform of the federal job training role. In effect, WIA combines the Employment Service with the second chance job training (i.e., JTPA) system and places both under the direction of local private-sector-led boards. Basically, WIA provides core labor market exchange services to all individuals and will provide education and training services to individuals who are currently not employable. Core services will be highly automated; individuals will enter their background and experience into a database, which can be searched by employers; and employers will enter job listings into a national database such as America's Job Bank. When someone is deemed not employable, the local WIA agency will work with that person to direct him or her into appropriate education and training opportunities. The legislation requires local workforce boards to use a system of vouchers (Individual Training Accounts) to finance the education and training. However, with a voucher system in place, it is unclear to what extent program administrators will be able to direct individuals into appropriate education and training opportunities through incentives, information, or sanctions.

The WIA has engendered considerable interest from the policy community. It is a non-incremental policy change that many believe has the potential to improve both the Employment Service and job training functions of the federal government. As discussed below, we believe that in order to achieve that potential, Congress needs to fund WIA at a significantly greater level. Nevertheless, in theory, local private-sector-led workforce boards should do a better job of enabling local programs to meet local labor market demands.

Furthermore, if employers and job-seekers do increase their usage and reliance on the public labor market exchange and job training system, then informal mechanisms with their informational imperfections (and discrimination) may fade in importance. It is important for African Americans and others who advocate for minority workers to get involved with their local workforce boards and, at the very least, monitor their actions.

Public assistance programs. Virtually since their inception, public assistance programs in this country have struggled with the issue of minimizing the financial assistance that goes to people who are capable of working. The Aid to Families with Dependent Children (AFDC) program had the Work Incentive (WIN) program, and it used implicit tax rates in its benefit formulas to encourage recipients to work. The Food Stamps program included the Food Stamps Employment and Training (FSET) program. In the 1980s, states were encouraged to try innovative methods to increase the number of public assistance recipients who entered the labor market. In 1988, Congress passed the Job Opportunity and Basic Skills (JOBS) legislation, based on some of the innovations that states or localities had tried during the early 1980s.[11] JOBS set strict guidelines about which clients must engage in employment or training and provided financial disincentives if states did not meet those guidelines.

Congress became impatient with the rate of progress of the JOBS program. In 1996 it passed the Personal Responsibility and Work Opportunity Reconciliation Act (PRWORA). This Act abolished AFDC and replaced it with Temporary Assistance to Needy Families (TANF), which provides for cash assistance that states may (no longer must) provide to economically distressed individuals. In addition, states have been given substantial increases in funds to use for childcare and health insurance (Medicaid). However, time limits have been established for how long individuals may receive cash benefits during their lifetime (five years), and states are reasonably unencumbered in their ability to enact rules or regulations that provide incentives for recipients to become employed or sanctions for those who don't. Dramatic caseload reductions have occurred in most states since this Act was passed, although it is unclear how much of the reduction was caused by the Act and how much was caused by robust national economic performance. Furthermore, there is little evidence about the extent of skills development for TANF recipients who have become employed.

State and local programs in the second chance system. States and local government agencies typically administer the second chance programs for the federal government, and their role is mostly concerned with management and administrative efficiency. This role should not be underemphasized.[12] Some states have substantial supplemental second chance programs. For example, California operates the Employment Training Panel program, which is funded by a supplemental unemployment insurance tax on employers. Ten states fund customized training programs through supplemental unemployment insurance assessments. The California program supports training that is targeted on retaining workers or employing workers who have been displaced.

While the thrust of welfare reform under PRWORA is immediate work assignment, Florida has implemented a program with a modest enrollment to promote education and training of welfare recipients at the state's community colleges and technical institutes.[13] Called the Performance Based Incentive Funding (PBIF) Program, it has several aspects that merit interest. It is targeted on occupations that have been identified as growing and in demand in Florida. Furthermore, it offers the training institutions financial incentives for redirecting curriculum to meet the needs of low-income students, having clients complete a program or degree, and placing recipients in a targeted occupation.

Finally, state and local governments engage in economic development activities that have substantial implications for skills development. Economic development assistance to firms often takes the form of customized training subsidies.[14] The National Governors' Association (NGA) estimated that in 1999 the states would spend more than $600 million on employer-focused job training programs. The NGA report, based on a recent survey of states, suggests that there are several trends in customized training, including the following:

- targeting existing firms and workers;
- funding training in generic skills that are transferable to other employers;
- targeting larger manufacturing firms;
- providing multi-firm projects; and
- maintaining relatively weak links to federal job training programs and state adult education programs.

These trends suggest that states are attempting to minimize the extent to which they are subsidizing training that benefits only the employers who receive the subsidy. Targeting existing firms and workers implies that states are willing to subsidize economic activity that will stem potential declines. Funding training in generic skill areas promotes the transferability of these skills and thus potential spillover benefits to other employers. Targeting manufacturing firms comes from an export-based strategy of economic growth that stimulates the entire region.

In the arsenal of state and local economic development tools, customized training is perhaps the mechanism most explicitly aimed at skills development. Its goal, like those of the other mechanisms, is to promote the economic growth of a whole region. The impacts of faster economic growth in a locality are generally progressive, as Timothy Bartik has argued in another paper.[15] Furthermore, the effects disproportionately favor blacks and less-educated workers.

Skills Development Policy Demonstrations and Experiments

Researchers and evaluators generally decry the reduced investment in policy experiments that seems to have occurred in the U.S. over the past two decades. However, there have been a number of interesting and innovative experiments or demonstrations of policies or practices aimed at skills development, from which valuable lessons have been learned.

One major initiative of this kind was a recent assessment of career academies. In a random assignment experiment, the Manpower Demonstration Research Corporation (MDRC) established and monitored the performance and outcomes of 10 career academies across the country. James Kemple and his colleagues reported that career academies are resulting in more and higher-quality career development experiences for students who attend the academies throughout high school (only about half of those who enroll last until 12th grade) and particularly for those who attend the more highly structured academies.[16]

The Quantum Opportunity Program has operated in four urban areas to retain at-risk youth in high school. This program relies on peer support and a "tough love" mentor/case manager on site to advocate for program participants. Evaluative evidence has shown it to have favorable impacts on both high school completion and decreased teen pregnancy.

The career academy experiment and the Quantum Opportunity Program are testing interventions that are housed in secondary schools in the first chance system. A number of experiments and demonstrations have attempted to improve the skills of disadvantaged adults through the second chance system. An approach that has received considerable publicity is identified as "sectoral":

Second-chance agencies and economic development policymakers in an area target an industrial sector for employment and training opportunities. In partnership with employers in the sector, the programs direct job-seekers into jobs and training in that sector or its supply chain.

Among training interventions, the Center for Employment Training (CET), founded in San Jose, California, has perhaps the best record of success.[17] In the JobStart Demonstration, CET produced some of the highest earnings gains ever, more than $8,000 (in 1998 dollars) for participants during the second and third year after training. CET's original mission was to address the employment problems of displaced Chicano farmworkers. From its inception, CET received strong support from Silicon Valley employers, and it was helped considerably by the fast growth and labor shortages of these firms. In the 1990s, the U.S. Department of Labor sponsored a large-scale replication of the CET program in many other cities across the nation.

CET's training model includes the following features:

- Strong connections with specific industries in the design and implementation of the program; this collaboration enables the identification of occupations with entry-level jobs that have good career prospects and expanding local demand.
- Instructors who have experience in the industry and occupation for which they provide training.
- Job developers who not only find jobs for graduates, but also develop long-term relationships with local firms.
- Short-term but intense training: Training on average is provided for 8 hours a day, 5 days a week for 30 weeks.
- Open-door policy: There is no screening of participants.
- Training that has open entry and open exit: Individuals start training any time there is an opening, and they stop training when they have demonstrated competency in the occupation.
- Training that resembles a workplace: Trainees punch in, are expected to be on time, and take breaks at specific times. Instructors deal with attendance and other problems as if the training period were a real job.
- Training that is integrated and contextual: Rather than basic literacy and math training first, followed by skills training, trainees start training for a

specific occupation from day one, with basic literacy skills taught as needed. Individualized training plans are developed for each trainee.

• Social adjustment treated as an important issue. Instructors seek to address social as well as skills needs of the trainees and provide counseling and mentoring as needed.

Project Quest, in San Antonio, is another highly promising training program.[18] Although it has not been subject to an evaluation using random assignment, evidence suggests it is highly successful. Before-and-after comparisons of Quest trainees suggest annual earnings gains of more than $4,000 (in 1995 dollars).[19] Case studies of individual trainees show specific actions taken by Quest counselors to help trainees over serious barriers to employment. Interviews with community college personnel and employers give high ratings to Quest's efforts to provide more support to trainees while making training more relevant to employers' needs.

Project Quest began operation in 1993; it was organized by two community-based organizations, both affiliated with the Industrial Area Foundations, an organization originally set up by the famed Chicago-based community organizer Saul Alinsky. The impetus for Project Quest came from the announcement in 1990 that Levi-Strauss was closing a plant in San Antonio that employed a thousand workers.

Project Quest's important features include:

• Targeted occupations identified in consultation with area employers to forecast future employment needs. Training curricula are customized for specific occupations to better meet the skills needs of employers.

• In some cases, Quest has led to newly defined occupations and restructured wages. For example, Quest conversations with employers led to a training program for banks in a new occupation entitled "financial customer services." Quest conversations with hospitals led to enhancements of the training for health unit clerk and some wage increases for this position.

• Quest training is provided by local community colleges. However, Quest intervention led the community colleges to extensively redesign the training to better fit what employers wanted.

- At an average of 17 months, Quest training is long-term compared to most government training programs for low-income persons.
- The community organizations running Quest recruit participants. Participants must have a high school diploma or GED and minimum math and reading scores.
- Quest provides a modest stipend for participants during training. The stipend allows trainees to support themselves during training with only part-time work.
- Quest provides extensive support mechanisms for participants both during and after training. Quest counselors tutor trainees, help them deal with teachers and employers, assist in pulling together financial support during training, provide personal advice and mentoring, and lead mandatory weekly peer group sessions.

A final demonstration project of interest is the Career Management Account (CMA) Demonstration. In anticipation of the WIA, the U.S. Department of Labor sponsored a multi-site project to test a voucher-like approach for directing job-seekers to education and training opportunities. In 13 sites across the country, the CMA Demonstration delivered voucher-style, customer-oriented services to dislocated workers eligible for JTPA training through Title III (EDWAA). The results of an evaluation of this demonstration suggested that it had positive results on employment outcomes, although the results were not strong statistically. The evaluators made many process recommendations, which should provide valuable insights as the local workforce boards across the country begin implementation of WIA.

What Works?

Certain characteristics seem to correlate with effectiveness of skills development programs, according to research and analyses of skill development programs. These characteristics can be categorized into content, training method, and program administration.

Content. The most important factors concerning content are ensuring that (1) the training is aimed toward occupations that are in demand in the local labor market, and (2) the training delivers basic academic skills and soft employability skills, as appropriate. It is important for training administrators to have mechanisms in place to help them determine occupations and skills in demand in their locality. They need to collaborate with local employers who can report skill deficiencies in new hires and identify business trends that may cause changes in occupational demands. In addition, training agencies can rely on the state or federal labor market information systems such as O*NET.

There are three broad categories of skills: specific skills, basic academic skills, and soft employability skills. It is important that education and training opportunity teach or reinforce the latter two types of skills. While most employers have come to recognize the value of these skills, many believe that they're even more important than specific technical skills. For one thing, technical skills often require a sound foundation in mathematics or technology. Second, teaching and learning cannot take place without communication and personal interaction. Third, employability skills and basic academic skills are valuable in themselves: There are few forms of employment in which the workers operate in isolation; most employees need communication and social skills, as well as the ability to work with others.

The CET program in San Jose, California, successfully integrated the basic and soft employability skills with more technical skills. This pedagogy was probably successful because it placed the academic skill training within the context of the technical skills training, and because it didn't require trainees to wait to get their technical training. Often, in the second chance system in particular, trainees are not future-oriented, and they get impatient with the linear school model that builds sequentially.

Training method. Some training methods appear to be more successful than others. In particular, many youth development programs emphasize the importance of a caring, adult mentor who develops a close relationship with the young people he or she mentors and has high expectations for them.

Adequate support mechanisms for trainees are also important elements of the delivery of programs.[20] Resources will obviously limit what can be accomplished, but the spectrum of possible support mechanisms that facilitate training is wide. If trainees are parents, childcare may be an important issue. If the training opportunity involves distant work or training sites, transportation may be an issue. If the training is conducted by a public agency for individuals before they are employed, or while they are unemployed, there may be questions of liability or other worker protection issues, such as safety, discrimination, or harassment. It is incumbent upon training agencies to ensure that these issues and their implications are clearly understood by trainees and by employers who provide work sites. Vocational guidance is another important element of training. Trainees need to have reliable information about the skill and training requirements of occupations, as well as the career payoffs that can be expected.

Program administration. The final training program characteristic is in the area of administrative practices. First, effective training requires substantial resources. In other words, there is no such thing as a free lunch. Among second chance programs for youth, Supported Work and Job Corps have been shown to have positive outcomes, whereas most other skills development initiatives for youth have had, at best, lackluster outcomes. But Supported Work[21] and Job Corps are intensive programs and thus quite expensive on a per participant basis. Among adult programs, CET has garnered considerable acclaim for its success, but it too is relatively costly compared to other programs. Furthermore, the training in Project Quest lasts 17 months. In short, we believe that in this area, you get what you pay for.

A second requirement for success is good leadership: Without the involvement of an individual with vision and leadership who will champion the program, success is unlikely. California implemented a welfare reform program titled, Greater Avenues for Independent (GAIN), in the latter half of the 1980s. A rigorous evaluation of GAIN in six counties showed that it was particularly effective in Riverside County. California's GAIN implementation in Riverside succeeded largely because of the commitment and dedication of its leadership. Similarly, the success of other programs has often been traced to the individual program administrators.

Accountability is also key. Many social programs have adopted the principles and practices that are used in industry, particularly manufacturing, in order to achieve continuous improvement. Performance standards are being used to ensure that the programs are accountable to taxpayers or other funders. But performance standards will be counter-productive unless they include important, measurable outcomes. Nevertheless, it seems apparent that program administrators are responsive to incentives that are tied to performance standards.

In summary, if policymakers want to support an effective system for skills development, they should make sure that it contains the following characteristics:

- The system offers training/educational opportunities that engender skills that are or will be in demand within the labor market area.

- The training/educational opportunities do not focus solely on specific technical skills.

- Training and education integrate basic skills, employability skills, and technical skills and deliver curriculum that is tailored to the learners' context.
- Adequate support mechanisms are available to enable participants to benefit fully from the skills development system.
- When training and educational opportunities are targeted on youth, there are caring, trained adult mentors.
- The system is adequately funded; programs that serve a few participants intensively are likely to have greater efficacy than programs that invest meagerly in a large number of people.
- The system relies on visionary leaders at the local level who have clear ideas of the mission and who can motivate staff and participants.
- The system uses performance standards for assessment and diagnostic purposes to provide accountability.

WIA's Likelihood of Success

WIA is the latest public policy attempt to direct skills development in this country. How does it measure up to our list of key elements of success? For some of these elements, WIA seems to be right on target, but for others, it is deficient and therefore unlikely to succeed.

Will the skills that are developed be in demand within the local labor market? One of the primary operating principles of WIA is control by local workforce boards that are led by the private sector. This suggests that the mechanism will be in place to identify skills that are in demand. Furthermore, the workforce boards and service providers will have access to O*NET and America's Job Bank, both of which will provide considerable information on skills and labor market demands. On the other hand, WIA operates on a system of vouchers (Individual Training Accounts) that will presumably give clients considerable latitude in their choice of education and training. Local administrators may have valid data on skills in demand, and they may have identified education and training opportunities in those areas, but unless appropriate mechanisms are set up to direct clients into those opportunities, they may opt for training that is not in demand.

Will the education and training opportunities under WIA integrate specific skill training, academic skills, and employability skills? The local workforce board will identify the programs that will be eligible for training. Thus, it will have the opportunity to use skill integration as a criterion in certifying institutions. This will require knowledgeable individuals to do the training certification process, and it may be open to local politics, if some local institutions are not certified.

Will WIA allow for adequate support mechanisms? Immediate work activity is its highest priority. Skills development through education and training will be available to a limited number of individuals. The one-stop systems that are being developed to implement WIA will provide core services to all individuals who encounter the system, but core services will involve only minimal support. Individuals will have access to job listings, presumably through electronic listings as well as hard-copy listings that may be posted for local opportunities, and they will be able to submit resumes electronically. Those who don't find a job after core services may be eligible for some further help depending on the resources and priorities of the local workforce board.

The first level of assistance for individuals who remain unemployed is called intensive services. These comprise job search assistance and counseling. If intensive services do not lead to employment, individuals may receive training services (i.e., vouchers for employment-related education or training). Thus, intensive or training services will provide some level of support to job seekers, but relatively few individuals will receive these services because of the meager funding that is being proposed.

On the other hand, with local control and with local business leaders and representatives from community-based organizations on the workforce boards, collaborative arrangements may spring up that facilitate referrals to other agencies and that provide for adequate support mechanisms. Furthermore, welfare reform under PRWORA has significantly increased childcare assistance and has made Medicaid available, for a limited period of time, to TANF recipients who will be in the labor force.

Will WIA be adequately funded? The JTPA system served only a fraction of individuals who would have been eligible for it and, similarly, the Employment Service was used by only a fraction of the employers looking for workers and workers looking for employment. WIA consolidates these two systems (along with other programs) but provides fewer resources than the two systems had individually. Furthermore, projections suggest that WIA will attract a larger number of employers and job-seekers. In short, WIA is not likely to have adequate resources unless it leverages significant levels of resources from other public or private sources. Without supplemental funds, it simply will not have the kinds of per-participant resources needed to successfully serve clients in second chance systems, such as CET, Project Quest, or Job Corps.

Will WIA have visionary leadership at the local level? Clearly the success of WIA at the local level will depend on the leadership of the workforce board and the administering agencies. There will be opportunities for leaders to emerge and, furthermore, the dramatic nature of the policy change will be best suited to individuals who are innovative and creative. Although resources will be incredibly thin, it is vital that some of those resources be invested in the professional development of local board members, administrators, and case staff.

Will WIA use performance measures to enhance accountability? Considerable effort and thought have been put into the issue of performance measures for WIA. This is clearly one element of program administration that will be put into effect, and it is our expectation that the performance measures will tailor the delivery of services.

CONCLUSIONS AND IMPLICATIONS

The major thrusts in skills development policy have been accountability, market-driven choice, decentralization/devolution, emphasis on immediate work, private-sector leadership, and consolidation. The policy characteristics that are in disfavor seem to be eligibility set-asides, process regulations, service delivery by administrative agencies, subsidized education and training, technical assistance, and research and development.

Current public policy in the area of skills development may be characterized as a grand experiment. Programs have evolved from a system that is top-down and centralized with regulatory protections and concern about equal access to a system that is wide-open and decentralized, operated largely by state bureaucrats and peopled by individuals at the local level who happen to take an interest and who happen to know the right individuals at the right time. Theoretical arguments can be made that the newer system will be more efficient and more equitable, but counter-arguments can be offered that the system will result in outcomes that are highly varied across localities.

African Americans have an important stake in this grand experiment. The greater emphasis on accountability could help black students if it changes expectations, or it could hurt them if the tools of assessment are racially biased. The greater emphasis on market-based choice also offers both opportunities and increased risks. As urban residents, African Americans will be disproportionately affected by the success or failure of charter schools and voucher programs. The greater emphasis on decentralization could improve access to labor market information if advocates for African American and other minority workers become involved in local workforce boards.

In the 21st century, the success of public policy in delivering efficient and equitable skills development depends on two key factors: (1) the extent to which WIA administrators can develop reliable outcome information on local training opportunities and provide it to clients in a way that influences their choices, and (2) the extent to which the work situations that TANF and other WIA clients find themselves in — as a result of the policies' push toward immediate work activity — will allow them to make progress in their skills and careers.

* * *

The authors gratefully thank Margaret Simms and Cecilia Conrad for their comments and suggestions. They also thank the discussants at the conference, Sheila Ards of Benedict College, Anthony Carnevale of the Educational Testing Service, Glenda Partee of the American Youth Policy Forum, and Steven Savner of CLASP.

NOTES

1. Robert H. Haveman and Barbara L. Wolfe, "Schooling and Economic Well-Being: The Role of Nonmarket Effects," *Journal of Human Resources* 19, no. 3: 377-407.

2. W. Norton Grubb, "Learning and Earning in the Middle: The Economic Benefits of Sub-Baccalaureate Education," Occasional paper, Community College Research Center, Institute on Education and the Economy, Columbia University, April 1999.

3. John F. Witte, "Achievement Effects of the Milwaukee Voucher Program" (University of Wisconsin at Madison, Madison, WI, January 1997, mimeographed); Jay P. Greene, Paul E. Peterson, and Jiangtao Du, "The Effectiveness of School Choice: The Milwaukee Experiment," Harvard University Education Policy and Governance Occasional Paper 97-1 (Harvard University, Cambridge, MA, March 1997); Cecilia Elena Rouse, "Private School Vouchers and Student Achievement: An Evaluation of the Milwaukee Parental Choice Program," *Quarterly Journal of Economics* 113, no. 2 (May 1998): 553-602; and this volume.

4. Christopher Jencks and Meredith Phillips, eds., *The Black-White Test Score Gap* (Washington, DC: The Brookings Institution, 1998).

5. Ronald F. Ferguson, "Teachers' Perceptions and Expectations and the Black-White Test Score Gap," in Jencks and Phillips, *The Black-White Test Score Gap.*

6. Christopher Jencks, "Racial Bias in Testing," in Jencks and Phillips, *The Black-White Test Score Gap.*

7. Jerry Horn and Gary Miron, "Evaluation of the Michigan Public School Academy Initiative," Final Report (The Evaluation Center, Western Michigan University, January 1999); University of California, Los Angeles, "Beyond the Rhetoric of Charter School Reform: A Study of Ten California School Districts," UCLA Charter School Study (Los Angeles, CA, 1999).

8. Lauren B. Resnick and M.W. Hall, "Learning Organizations for Sustainable Education Reform." *Daedelus* 127, 89–118, 1998.

9. Eli Ginzberg, "MDTA and CETA," in *Of Heart and Mind: Social Policy Essays in Honor of Sar A. Levitan*, ed. Garth Mangum and Stephen Mangum (Kalamazoo, MI: W.E. Upjohn Institute for Employment Research, 1996).

10. Ginzberg, "MDTA and CETA."

11. Judith M. Gueron and Edward Pauly, *From Welfare to Work* (New York: Russell Sage Foundation, 1991).

12. Eugene Bardach, *Improving the Productivity of JOBS Programs* (New York: Manpower Demonstration Research Corporation, 1993).

13. Brandon Roberts and Jeffrey D. Padden, *Welfare to Wages: Strategies to Assist the Private Sector to Employ Welfare Recipients*, vol. 2 (Flint, MI: Mott Foundation, 1998).

14. Timothy J. Bartik, *Who Benefits from State and Local Economic Development Policies?* (Kalamazoo, MI: W.E. Upjohn Institute for Employment Research, 1991); National Governors' Association, *A Comprehensive Look at State-Funded, Employer-Focused Job Training Programs* (Washington, DC: National Governors' Association, 1999).

15. Bartik, *Who Benefits from State and Local Economic Development Policies?*

16. James J. Kemple, Susan M. Poglinco, and Jason C. Snipes, "Career Academies: Building Career Awareness and Work-Based Learning Activities Through Employer Partnerships" (New York: MDRC, 1999).

17. The description of this program is largely based on Edwin Meléndez, *Working on Jobs: The Center for Employment Training* (Boston: The Mauricio Gastón Institute for Latino Community Development and Public Policy, 1996).

18. The main source for this description is Brenda A. Lautsch and Paul Osterman, "Changing the Constraints: A Successful Employment and Training Strategy," in *Jobs and Economic Development: Strategies and Practice*, ed. Robert P. Giloth (Thousand Oaks, CA: Sage Publications, 1998), pp. 204–233.

19. Lautsch and Osterman explain this calculation as the increased probability of working (24.5 percent) times the average weekly hours in a post-Quest job (39.3 hours) times the average wage in a post-Quest job ($8.41) times 50 weeks per year. The pre-Quest average annual earnings (for those employed) were $9,700 (1995 dollars) for 50 weeks of employment.

20. Kevin Hollenbeck and Bridget F. Timmeney, "School-to-Work Transition Programs," in *School Social Work Practice and Research Perspectives*, ed. Robert Constable, John P. Flynn, and Shirley McDonald (Chicago: Lyceum Books, 1996), pp. 237–252.

21. Robinson G. Hollister Jr., Peter Kemper, and Rebecca A. Maynard, eds., *The National Supported Work Demonstration* (Madison, WI: University of Wisconsin Press, 1984).

Chapter 1. Introduction and Overview, by Cecilia A. Conrad

Frazis, Harley, Maury Gittleman, Michael Horrigan, and Mary Joyce. "Results from the 1995 Survey of Employer-Provided Training." *Monthly Labor Review*, June 1998 (vol. 121, no. 6).

National Center for Education Statistics. *Digest of Education Statistics, 1999.* (Accessed at http://nces.ed.gov/pubs2000/digest99)

Schochet, Peter. "National Job Corps Study: Characteristics of Youths Served by Job Corps." Mathematica Policy Research, Inc. (Submitted to U.S. Department of Labor Employment and Training Administration, Office of Policy and Research, DOL Contract No. K-4279-3-00-80-3, January 15, 1998).

Social Policy Research Associates. "PY 97 SPIR Data Book" (Prepared for the Office of Policy and Research, Employment and Training Administration, U.S. Department of Labor, DOL Contract No. K-5950-6-00-80-30, June 1, 1999).

U.S. Department of Education, National Center for Education Statistics (NCES). "Later Completions by Dropouts." Accessed from the NCES web site December 2000.

Chapter 2. "The Effect of Class Size and School Vouchers on Minority Achievement," by Cecilia Elena Rouse

Angrist, J., G. Imbens, and D. Rubin. "Identification of Causal Effects Using Instrumental Variables." *Journal of the American Statistical Association*, vol. 91, no. 434 (1996).

Angrist, Joshua, and Victor Lavy. "Using Maimonides' Rule to Estimate the Effect of Class Size on Children's Academic Achievement." *Quarterly Journal of Economics,* vol. 114, no. 2 (May 1999):

Bagley, Carl, Philip Woods, and Ron Glatter. "Barriers to School Responsiveness in the Education Quasi-Market." *School Organisation,* vol. 16, no. 1 (1996).

Barrow, Lisa, and Cecilia Elena Rouse. "Using Market Valuation to Assess Public School Spending." National Bureau of Economic Research Working Paper No. 9054 (July 2002).

Boozer, Michael A., and Cecilia Elena Rouse. "Intra-School Variation in Class Size: Patterns and Implications." *Journal of Urban Economics,* vol. 50, no. 1 (July 2001).

Borland, Melvin V., and Roy M. Howsen. "Student Academic Achievement and the Degree of Market Concentration in Education." *Economics of Education Review, vol.* 11, no. 1 (1992).

Chubb, John E., and Terry M. Moe. *Politics, Markets, and America's Schools.* Washington, D.C.: The Brookings Institution, 1990.

Clancy, Dan, Charlie Toulmin, and Merry Bukolt. "Wisconsin Public School Finance Programs, 1993-94." In *Public School Finance Programs of the United States and Canada, 1993-94,* edited by Steven D. Gold, David M. Smith, and Stephen B. Lawton (New York: American Education Finance Association, 1995).

Evans, William N., and Robert M. Schwab. "Finishing High School and Starting College: Do Catholic Schools Make a Difference?" *Quarterly Journal of Economics,* no.110 (November 1995).

Figlio, David N., and Joe A. Stone. "Are Private Schools Really Better?" *Research in Labor Economics,* 1999.

Finn, Jeremy D., and Charles M. Achilles. "Answers and Questions About Class Size: A Statewide Experiment," *American Educational Research Journal,* vol. 27, no. 3 (Fall 1990).

Folger, John, and Carolyn Breda. "Evidence from Project STAR About Class Size and Student Achievement." *Peabody Journal of Education* 67 (1989).

Frey, Donald E. "Can Privatizing Education Really Improve Achievement? An Essay Review." *Economics of Education Review,* vol. 11, no. 4 (1992).

Friedman, Milton. *Capitalism and Freedom.* Chicago: University of Chicago Press, 1992.

Garner, W.T., and Jane Hannaway. "Private Schools: The Client Connection." *In Family Choice in Schooling,* edited by M. Manley-Casimir (Lexington, MA: D.C. Heath, 1992).

Greene, Jay P., and Daryl Hall. "The CEO Horizon Scholarship Program: A Case Study of School Vouchers in the Edgewood Independent School District, San Antonio, Texas." Mathematica Policy Research Inc. Final Report (May 2001).

Greene, Jay P., William G. Howell, and Paul E. Peterson. "An Evaluation of the Cleveland Scholarship Program." Program on Education Policy and Governance, Harvard University mimeo, September 1997.

Greene, Jay P., Paul E. Peterson, and Jiangtao Du. "The Effectiveness of School Choice: The Milwaukee Experiment," Harvard University Education Policy and Governance Occasional Paper 97-1, March 1997.

Hanushek, Eric A. "Conclusions and Controversies About the Effectiveness of School Resources," *Economic Policy Review*, vol. 4, no. 1 (March 1998).

Heckman, James, and Jeffrey Smith. "Assessing the Case for Randomized Evaluation of Social Programs," in *Measuring Labour Market Measures: Evaluating the Effects of Active Labour Market Policies*, edited by Karsten Jensen and Per Kongshoj (Copenhagen: Ministry of Labour, 1993).

Howell, William G., and Paul B. Peterson, with Patrick J. Wolf and David E. Campbell. *The Education Gap: Vouchers and Urban Schools*. Washington, DC: The Brookings Institution Press, 2002.

Howell, William G., Patrick J. Wolf, Paul E. Peterson, and David E. Campbell. "Test-Score Effects of School Vouchers in Dayton, Ohio, New York City, and Washington, D.C.: Evidence from Randomized Field Trials." Program on Education Policy and Governance Working Paper (August, 2000).

Hoxby, Caroline M. "The Effects of Private School Vouchers on Schools and Students." In *Holding Schooling Accountable: Performance-Based Reform in Education*, edited by Helen F. Ladd (Washington, D.C.: The Brookings Institution, 1996).

Hoxby, Caroline M. "The Effects of Class Size and Composition on Student Achievement: New Evidence from Natural Population Variation." *Quarterly Journal of Economics*, vol. 128, no. 4 (2000).

Hoxby, Caroline M. "Does Competition Among Public Schools Benefit Students and Taxpayers? Evidence from National Variation in School Districting." *American Economic Review*, vol. 90, no. 5 (December 2000).

Krueger, Alan B. "Reassessing the View That American Schools Are Broken." *Economic Policy Review*, vol. 4, no. 1 (March 1998).

Krueger, Alan B. "Experimental Estimates of Education Production Functions." *Quarterly Journal of Economics*, vol. 114, no. 2 (May 1999).

Krueger, Alan B., and Diane M. Whitmore, "The Effect of Attending a Small Class in the Early Grades on College Test Taking and Middle School Test Results: Evidence from Project STAR." *Economic Journal*, vol. 111 (January 2001).

Krueger, Alan B., and Pei Zhu. "Another Look at the New York City School Voucher Experiment." *American Behavioral Scientist*, 2003 (forthcoming).

Milwaukee Public Schools. *Directions: Your School Selection Guide for the 1997-98 School Year*. Milwaukee Public Schools, 1997.

Murnane, Richard J. "A Review Essay—Comparisons of Public and Private Schools: Lessons from the Uproar." *Journal of Human Resources*, vol. 19 (1984).

Mayer, Daniel P., Paul Peterson, David E. Myers, Christina Clark Tuttle, and William G. Howell. "School Choice in New York City After Three Years: An Evaluation of the School Choice Scholarships Program." Mathematica Policy Research Inc. Final Report, February 2002.

Neal, Derek. "The Effects of Catholic Secondary Schooling on Educational Achievement." *Journal of Labor Economics*, vol. 15, no. 1. part 1 (January 1997).

Northwest Regional Educational Laboratory. *Catalog of School Reform Models: First Edition*, March 1998.

Peterson, Paul E., David Myers, and William G. Howell. "An Evaluation of the New York City School Choice Scholarships Program: The First Year." Program on Education Policy and Governance, PEPG 98-12, 1998.

Peterson, Paul E., David Myers, and William G. Howell. "An Evaluation of the Horizon Scholarship Program in the Edgewood Independent School District, San Antonio, Texas: The First Year," Mathematica Policy Research and Program on Education Policy and Governance Working Paper, 1999.

Rouse, Cecilia Elena. "Private School Vouchers and Student Achievement: An Evaluation of the Milwaukee Parental Choice Program." *Quarterly Journal of Economics*, vol. 113, no. 2 (May 1998).

Rouse, Cecilia Elena. "Schools and Student Achievement: More on the Milwaukee Parental Choice Program." *Economic Policy Review*, vol. 4 no. 1 (March 1998).

Stecher, Brian M., and George W. Bohrnstedt. "Class Size Reduction in California: Early Evaluation Findings, 1996-98." CSR Research Consortium Technical Report, June 1999.

U.S. Department of Education. "A Study of Charter Schools: First Year Report." http://wws.ed.gov/pubs/charter, May 1997.

U.S. Department of Education, National Center for Education Statistics. *Digest of Education Statistics* 1998, http://nces.ed.gov/pubs99/digest98, 1998.

Wexler, Edward, JoAnn Izu, Lisa Carlos, Bruce Fuller, Gerald Hayward, and Mike Kirst. "California's Class Size Reduction: Implications for Equity, Practice, and Implementation." WestEd Technical Report, March 1998.

Wirt, John, Tom Snyder, Jennifer Sable, Susan P. Choy, Yupin Bae, Janis Stennet, Allison Gruner, and Marianne Perie. *The Condition of Education*, 1998 (NCES

98-013). Washington, D.C.: U.S. Department of Education, National Center for Education Statistics: 1998.

Witte, John F. "Achievement Effects of the Milwaukee Voucher Program." University of Madison mimeo, January 1997.

Witte, John F., Christopher A. Thorn, Kim M. Pritchard, and Michele Claibourn. "Fourth-Year Report: Milwaukee Parental Choice Program." University of Wisconsin mimeo, December 1994.

Witte, John F., Troy D. Sterr, and Christopher A. Thorn. "Fifth-Year Report: Milwaukee Parental Choice Program." University of Wisconsin mimeo, December 1995.

Word, Elizabeth, J. Johnston, Helen Bain, et al. "The State of Tennessee's Student/Teacher Achievement Ratio (STAR) Project: Technical Report 1985-1990." Nashville: Tennessee State Department of Education, 1990.

Chapter 3. "The Digital Divide in Educating Black Students and Workers," by Alan B. Krueger

Anderson, Ronald, Vicki Lundmark, Linda Harris, and Shon Magnan. "Equity in Computing." In Chuck Huff and Thomas Finholt (eds.), *Social Issues in Computing* (New York: McGraw-Hill, Inc., 1994).

Angrist, Joshua, and Victor Lavy. "New Evidence on Classroom Computers and Pupil Learning." Mimeo., Massachusetts Institute of Technology (Cambridge, MA, May 1999).

Autor, David H. "Why Do Temporary Help Firms Provide Free General Skills Training?" Unpublished dissertation chapter, Harvard University, 1999.

Autor, David, Lawrence Katz, and Alan Krueger. "Computing Inequality: Have Computers Changed the Labor Market?" *Quarterly Journal of Economics*, vol. 113, No. 4 (November 1998).

Becker, Henry. "How Schools Use Microcomputers: Summary of the 1983 National Survey." In *Second National Survey of Instructional Uses of School Computers* (The Johns Hopkins University, Baltimore, MD).

Becker, Henry, and Carleton Sterling. "Equity in School Computer Use: National Data and Neglected Considerations." *Journal of Educational Computing Research*, vol. 3, no. 3 (1987).

Boozer, Michael, Alan Krueger, and Shari Wolkon. "Race and School Quality Since *Brown* vs. *Board of Education*." In *Brookings Papers on Economic Activity: Microeconomics*, edited by Martin N. Baily and Clifford Winston (1992).

Cuban, Larry, and Heather Kirkpatrick. "Computers Make Kids Smarter— Right?" *Technos*, vol. 7 no. 2 (Summer 1998).

DiNardo, John, and Jorn-Steffen Pischke. "The Returns to Computer Use Revisited: Have Pencils Changed the Wage Structure Too?" *Quarterly Journal of Economics*, February 1997.

Holzer, Harry. "Employer Skill Needs and Labor Market Outcomes." (Mimeo, Michigan State University, September 1995).

Holzer, Harry. *What Employers Want.* New York: Russell Sage Foundation, 1996.

Krueger, Alan. "How Computers Have Changed the Wage Structure: Evidence From Microdata, 1984-1989." *Quarterly Journal of Economics*, vol. 108, no. 1, (February 1993).

Kulik, Chen-Lin, and James Kulik. "Effectiveness of Computer-Based Instruction: An Updated Analysis." In *Computers in Human Behavior*, vol. 7 (1991).

McPhail, Irving. "Computer Inequities in School Uses of Microcomputers: Policy Implications." *Journal of Negro Education*, vol. 54, no. 1 (1985).

Ragosta, Marjorie, Paul Holland, and Dean Jamison. "Computer-Assisted Instruction and Compensatory Education: The ETS/LAUSD Study." Final Report, Princeton, NJ, Educational Testing Service, April 1982.

United States Commerce Department, National Telecommunications and Information Administration. *Falling Through the Net: Defining the Digital Divide.* Washington, D.C., July 1999.

Wenglinsky, Harold. "Does it Compute? The Relationship Between Educational Technology and Student Achievement in Mathematics." Unpublished paper for the Policy Information Center, Research Division, Educational Testing Service, Princeton, NJ, September 1998.

Chapter 4. "Racial and Ethnic Differences in the Impact of Job Training on Wages," by William M. Rodgers, III

Altonji, Joseph G., and James R. Spletzer. "Worker Characteristics, Job Characteristics, and the Receipt of On-the-Job Training." *Industrial and Labor Relations Review* 45 (1991).

Boozer, Michael A., Alan B. Krueger, and Shari Wolkon. "Race and School Quality since *Brown* vs. *Board of Education*." In *Brookings Papers on Economic Activity Microeconomics*, edited by Martin N. Baily and Clifford Winston (1992).

Bound, John, and Richard B. Freeman. "What Went Wrong? The Erosion of Relative Earnings and Employment Among Young Black Men in the 1980's." *The Quarterly Journal of Economics* 107 (February 1992).

Corcoran, Mary, and Greg J. Duncan. "Work History, Labor Force Attachment, and Earnings Differences Between the Races and Sexes." *The Journal of Human Resources* 14 (1979).

Duncan, Greg J., and Saul Hoffman. "On-the-Job Training and Earnings Differences by Race and Sex." *Review of Economics and Statistics* 61 (November 1979).

Duncan, Kevin C. "The Vintage Schooling Hypothesis and Racial Differences in Earnings and On-the-Job Training: A Longitudinal Analysis." *The Review of Black Political Economy 20* (Winter 1992).

Ferguson, Ronald F. "New Evidence on the Growing Value of Skill and Consequences for Racial Disparity and Returns to Schooling." Unpublished paper, John F. Kennedy School of Government, Harvard University (September 1994).

Ferguson, Ronald F. "Shifting Challenges: Fifty Years of Economic Change Toward Black-White Earnings Equality." *Daedulus* 124 (Winter 1995).

Goldsmith, Arthur H., William Darity Jr., and Jonathan R. Veum. "Race, Cognitive Skills, Psychological Capital, and Wages." *Review of Black Political Economy,* vol. 26, no. 2 (Fall 1998).

Hausman, J., and W. Taylor. "Panel Data and Unobservable Individual Effects." *Econometrica* 49 (1981).

Juhn, Chinhui, Kevin Murphy, and Brooks Pierce. "Accounting for the Slowdown in Black-White Wage Convergence." In *Workers and Their Wages: Changing Patterns in the United States,* edited by M. Kosters (Washington, DC: AEI Press, 1991).

Lynch, Lisa M. "The Role of Off-the-Job vs. On-the-Job Training for the Mobility of Women Workers." *American Economic Review* 81 (1991).

Lynch, Lisa M. "Private-Sector Training and the Earnings of Young Workers." *American Economic Review* 82 (1992).

Mason, Patrick L. "Race, Culture, and Skill: Interracial Wage Differences Among African Americans, Latinos, and Whites." *The Review of Black Political Economy,* Winter 1997.

Maxwell, N. "The Effect on Black-White Wage Differences of Differences in the Quantity and Quality of Education." *Industrial and Labor Relations Review* 47 (January 1994).

Myers, Samuel, Jr. " 'The Rich Get Richer And' — The Problem of Race and Inequality in the 1990s." *Journal of Law and Inequality* 11(1993).

Neal, Derek A., and William R. Johnson. "The Role of Pre-Market Factors in Black-White Differences." *The Journal of Political Economy* 104 (1996).

O'Neill, June. "The Role of Human Capital in Earnings Differences Between Black and White Men." *The Journal of Economic Perspectives* 4 (Fall 1990).

Rodgers, William M. "Male Black-White Wage Gaps, 1979-1991: A Distributional Analysis." Unpublished paper, The College of William and Mary, 1997.

Rodgers, William M. "Male Sub-metropolitan Black-White Wage Gaps: New Evidence for the 1980s." *Urban Studies* 34 (1997).

Rodgers, William M., and William E. Spriggs. "What Does the AFQT Really Measure: Race, Wages, Schooling and the AFQT Score." *The Review of Black Political Economy* 24 (1996).

Rodgers, William M., and William E. Spriggs. "Accounting for the Racial Gap in AFQT Scores: Comment on Nan L. Maxwell, 'The Effect on Black-White Wage Differences of Differences in the Quantity and Quality of Education'." *Industrial and Labor Relations Review*, vol. 55, no. 3 (2002).

Schochet, Peter Z. "Alternatives to College Education: Incidence and Returns for Young Males." Unpublished Ph.D. dissertation, Yale University, 1991.

Sexton, Edwin A., and Reed N. Olsen. "The Returns to On-the-Job Training: Are They the Same for Blacks and Whites?" *The Southern Economic Journal* 61 (October 1994).

Veum, Jonathan R. "Sources of Training and Their Impact on Wages." *Industrial Labor Relations Review* 48 (July 1995).

Wilson, Beth A., and James P. Ziliak. "Pre-Market Factors and the Black-White Wage Gap: Evidence from Panel Data." Unpublished manuscript, Xavier University and University of Oregon, 1998.

Chapter 5. "Do Black Workers Lack Soft Skills?"- by Cecilia Conrad

Bongiorno, Lori. "Ivy and Innovation: B-Schools Try Harder." *Business Week*, June 7, 1993.

Cafasso, Rosemary. "Selling Your Soft Side (People Skills Win You the Job)." *Computerworld* 30 (April 1, 1996.).

Carnevale, Anthony Patrick. *America and the New Economy.* The American Society for Training and Development and the U.S. Department of Labor, Employment and Training Administration, 1991.

Conrad, Cecilia. *Soft Skills: A Guide for Informed Discussion.* Washington, DC: Joint Center for Political and Economic Studies, 1999.

Cornell, Bradford, and Ivo Welch. "Culture, Information, and Screening Discrimination." *Journal of Political Economy*, vol. 104 (1996).

Davis, Dwight B. "Hard Demand for Soft Skills." *Datamation* 39 (15 January, 1993).

Duncan, Greg J., and Rachel Dunifon. "Soft-Skills and Long-Run Labor Market Success." *Research in Labor Economics* 17 (1998).

England, Paula, Karen Christopher, and Lori L. Reid. "Gender, Race, Ethnicity, and Wages," in *Latinas and African American Women at Work: Race, Gender and Economic Inequality*, edited by Irene Brown (New York: Russell Sage Foundation, 1999).

Farkas, George, Paula England, Keven Vicknair, and Barbara Stanek Kilbourne, "Cognitive Skill, Skill Demands of Jobs, and Earnings Among Young European American, African American, and Mexican American Workers." *Social Forces* 75 (March 1997).

Ferguson, Ron, and Randall Filer. "Do Better Jobs Make Better Workers? Absenteeism from Work Among Inner-City Black Youths." In *The Black Youth Employment Crisis*, edited by Richard B. Freemand and Harry Holzer (Chicago: University of Chicago Press, 1986).

Fry, John P., and Paul G. Whitmore. "What Are Soft Skills?" Papers presented at the CONARC Soft Skills Conference, Fort Bliss, Texas, December 1972.

Gaustad, Virginia M. "Qualities and Skills Employers Like and Dislike in Clerical Workers: An Office Administration Survey." San Bernadino Community College District, Office of Planning and Research, 1988.

Georges, James C. "The Myth of Soft Skills Training." *Training* 33 (January 1996).

Gifford, Robert, Cheuk Fan Ng, and Margaret Wilkinson. "Nonverbal Cues in the Employment Interview: Links Between Applicant Qualities and Interviewer Judgements." *Journal of Applied Psychology*, vol. 70, no. 4 (1985).

Goldsmith, Arthur H., Jonathan R. Veum, and William A. Darity, Jr. "The Impact of Psychological and Human Capital and Wages." *Economic Inquiry* 35 (October 1997).

Heathman, Dena J., and Brian H. Kleiner. "Training and Technology: The Future Is Now." *Training and Development* 45 (September 1991).

Hershey, Alan M., Marsha K. Silverberg, Joshua Harrison, Paula Hudis, and Russell Jackson. *Expanding Options For Students: Report to Congress on the National Evaluation of School-to-Work Implementation*. Princeton, N.J.: Mathematica Policy Research, February 1999.

Hollenbeck, Kevin. "The Workplace Know-How Skills Needed to Be Productive." Technical Report prepared by The Upjohn Institute for Kalamazoo County Education for Employment Outcomes Task Force, May 1994.

Holzer, Harry. *What Employers Want: Job Prospects for Less-Educated Workers.* New York: Russell Sage Foundation, 1996.

Holzer, Harry. "Barriers to Higher Employment Rates Among African Americans." In *Job Creation: Prospects and Strategies*, edited by Wilhelmina A. Leigh and Margaret C. Simms (Washington DC: Joint Center for Political and Economic Studies, 1998).

Kirschenman, Joleen, and Kathryn M. Neckerman. "We'd Love to Hire Them, But...':The Meaning of Race for Employers." In *The Urban Underclass*, edited by Christopher Jencks and Paul E. Peterson (Washington, D.C.: The Brookings Institution, 1991).

Kirschenman, Joleen, Philip Moss, and Chris Tilly. "Employer Screening Methods and Racial Exclusion: Evidence from New In-Depth Interviews with Employers." New York: Russell Sage Foundation (September 1995) [available at http://epn.org/sage/rstikm.html, accessed October 1997; New location: http://www.russellsage.org/publications/working_papers.html]

Leigh, J. Paul, and John Lust. "Punctuality and Tardiness in Supplying Labor." *Atlantic Economic Journal* 14 (July 1986).

Leigh, J. Paul, and John Lust. "Determinants of Employee Tardiness." *Work and Occupations* 15 (February 1988).

Leigh, Wilhelmina A., Deitra H. Lee and Malinda A. Lindquist. *Soft Skills Training: An Annotated Guide to Selected Programs.* Washington, DC: Joint Center for Political and Economic Studies, 1999.

Lynch, Lisa M., and Sandra E. Black. *Beyond the Incidence of Training: Evidence form the National Employer Survey.* EQW Working Papers WP35. Philadelphia: University of Pennsylvania, 1996.

Maume, David J. Jr., A. Silvia Cancio, and T. David Evans. "Cognitive Skills and Racial Wage Inequality: Reply to Farkas and Vicknair." *American Sociological Review* 61 (August 1996).

Mead, Lawrence M. *The New Politics of Poverty: The Nonworking Poor in America.* New York: Basic Books, 1992.

Menagh, Melanie. "Made to Order." *Computerworld*, August 19, 1996.

Moss, Philip, and Chris Tilly. "Skills and Race in Hiring: Quantitative Findings From Face-To-Face Interviews." *Eastern Economic Journal, Summer* 1995.

Moss, Philip, and Chris Tilly. "Soft Skills and Race: An Investigation of Black Men's Employment Problems." *Work and Occupations* 23 (August 1996).

National Center for Education Statistics. "International Life Skills Survey" (1999). Accessed online at http:nces.ed.gov/ilss/

Rodgers, William M., and William E. Spriggs. "What Does the AFQT Really Measure: Race, Wages, Schooling and the AFQT Score." *Review of Black Political Economy* 24 (Spring 1996).

O'Neil, Harold F., Keith Alfred, and Eva L. Baker. "Measurement of Workforce Readiness: Review of Theoretical Frameworks," Research Paper, National Center for Research on Evaluation, Standards and Student Testing, 1993. (ERIC Document ED353328).

O'Neil, June. "The Role of Human Capital in Earnings Differences Between Black and White Men." *The Journal of Economic Perspectives* 4 (Fall 1990).

Parsons, Charles K. and Robert C. Liden. "Interviewer Perceptions of Applicant Qualifications: A Multivariate Field Study of Demographic Characteristics and Nonverbal Cues." *Journal of Applied Psychology*, vol. 69, no..4 (1984).

Petterson, Stephen M. "Are Young Black Men Really Less Willing to Work?" *American Sociological Review* 62 (August 1997).

Rossett, Allison, and Jeremy Barnett. "Designing Under the Influence (Need for Instructional Design Using Multimedia Systems)." *Training* 33 (December 1996).

Secretary's Commission on Achieving Necessary Skills (SCANS). "Learning a Living: A Blueprint for High Performance." U.S. Department of Labor (April 1992).

Sternberg, Robert J., Richard K. Wagner, Wendy M. Williams, and Joseph A. Horvath 2000, "Practical Cognition," Electronic Document. http://nces.ed.gov/ilss/documents/practcog.pdf. Retrieved June 23, 2000.

Strebler, Marie. "Soft Skills and Hard Questions." *People Management* 3 (29 May 1997)

Visher, Mary G. 1998. "School-to-Work in the 1990s: A Look at Programs and Practices in American High Schools."

Whitmore, Paul G. "The Behavioral Model as a Tool for Analyzing Soft Skills." Paper presented at CONARC Soft Skills Conference, Fort Bliss, Texas, December 1972.

Wilson, Linda. "Yearn to Learn." *Computerworld* (June 1997).

Wilson, William Julius. *When Work Disappears: The World of the New Urban Poor.* New York: Alfred A. Knopf, 1997.

Zwerling, Craig, and Hilary Silver. "Race and Job Dismissals in a Federal Bureaucracy." *American Sociological Review* 57 (October 1992).

Chapter 6. "The Role of Public Policy," by Timothy Bartik and Kevin Hollenbeck

Bardach, Eugene. *Improving the Productivity of JOBS Programs.* New York: Manpower Demonstration Research Corporation, 1993.

Bartik, Timothy J. *Who Benefits From State and Local Economic Development Policies?* Kalamazoo, MI: W.E. Upjohn Institute for Employment Research, 1991.

Ginzberg, Eli. "MDTA and CETA." In *Of Heart and Mind: Social Policy Essays in Honor of Sar A. Levitan,* edited by Garth Mangum and Stephen Mangum. Kalamazoo, MI: W.E. Upjohn Institute for Employment Research, 1996.

Greene, Jay P., Paul E. Peterson, and Jiangtao Du. "The Effectiveness of School Choice: The Milwaukee Experiment." Harvard University Education Policy and Governance Occasional Paper 97-1 (March 1997).

Grubb, W. Norton. *Learning and Earning in the Middle: The Economic Benefits of Sub-Baccalaureate Education.* Unpublished manuscript, 1998.

Gueron, Judith M., and Edward Pauly. From *Welfare to Work.* New York: Russell Sage Foundation, 1991.

Haveman, Robert H., and Barbara L. Wolfe. "Schooling and Economic Well-Being: The Role of Nonmarket Effects." *The Journal of Human Resources,* vol. 19, no. 3 (1984).

Hollenbeck, Kevin, and Bridget F. Timmeney. "School-to-Work Transition Programs." In *School Social Work Practice and Research Perspectives,* edited by Robert Constable, John P. Flynn, and Shirley McDonald. Chicago: Lyceum Books, Inc., 1996.

Hollister, Robinson G., Jr., Peter Kemper, and Rebecca A. Maynard, eds. *The National Supported Work Demonstration.* Madison, WI: The University of Wisconsin Press, 1984.

Horn, Jerry, and Gary Miron. "Evaluation of the Michigan Public School Academy Initiative." Final report. The Evaluation Center, Western Michigan University, January 1999.

Jencks, Christopher. "Racial Bias in Testing." In *The Black-White Test Score Gap,* edited by Christopher Jencks and Meredith Phillips. Washington: The Brookings Institution, 1998.

Jencks, Christopher, and Meredith Phillips, eds. *The Black-White Test Score Gap.* Washington: The Brookings Institution, 1998.

Kemple, James J., Susan M Poglinco, and Jason C Snipes. "Career Academies: Building Career Awareness and Work-Based Learning Activities Through Employer Partnerships." New York: Manpower Demonstration Research Corporation, 1999. Executive summary available at http://www.mdrc.org.

Lautsch, Brenda A., and Paul Osterman. "Changing the Constraints: A Successful Employment and Training Strategy." In *Jobs and Economic Development: Strategies and Practice*, edited by Robert P. Giloth. Thousand Oaks, CA: Sage Publications, 1988.

Meléndez, Edwin. *Working on Jobs: The Center for Employment Training*. Boston, MA: The Mauricio Gastón Institute for Latino Community Development and Public Policy, 1996.

National Governors Association. *A Comprehensive Look at State-Funded, Employer-Focused Job Training Programs*. Washington: National Governors Association, 1999.

Roberts, Brandon, and Jeffrey D. Padden. *Welfare to Wages: Strategies to Assist the Private Sector to Employ Welfare Recipients*, Vol. 2. Flint, MI: Mott Foundation, 1998.

Rouse, Cecilia Elena. "Private School Vouchers and Student Achievement: An Evaluation of the Milwaukee Parental Choice Program." *The Quarterly Journal of Economics*, May 1998.

U.S. Department of Labor, The Secretary's Commission on Achieving Necessary Skills (SCANS). "What Work Requires of Schools." Washington: U.S. Department of Labor, 1991.

University of California, Los Angeles, UCLA Charter School Study. "Beyond the Rhetoric of Charter School Reform: A Study of Ten California School Districts." Los Angeles: UCLA, 1999.

Witte, John F. "Achievement Effects of the Milwaukee Voucher Program." University of Wisconsin at Madison mimeo, January 1997.

Timothy J. Bartik

Timothy Bartik is senior economist at the W.E. Upjohn Institute, where he is responsible for developing and conducting research on state and local economic development and local labor markets. Currently he is researching alternative policies for increasing labor demand for the urban poor. He is the co-editor of Economic Development Quarterly and serves on the editorial boards of several journals of regional economics.

His recent publications include *Jobs for the Poor: Can Labor Demand Policies Help?* (Russell Sage Foundation and the Upjohn Institute, 2001) and "Examining the Effects of Industry Trends and Structure on Welfare Caseloads," (with Randall W. Eberts) in *Economic Conditions and Welfare Reform*, edited by Sheldon H. Danziger (Upjohn Institute, 1999). He holds a Ph.D. in economics from the University of Wisconsin-Madison.

Cecilia A. Conrad

Cecilia Conrad is the Stedman-Sumner professor of economics at Pomona College. Her recent projects include an analysis of trends in the economic status of minority women; a study of the market for science and technology workers; and an exploration of differences in the recruitment practices of minority and non-minority owned companies. She is currently engaged in a study of the causes and consequences of inequality in local public expenditure on children and families.

Conrad has authored numerous scholarly as well as popular articles, and has contributed research to numerous edited volumes, most recently in *America Becoming: Racial Trends and Their Consequences*, edited by Neil Smelser, William Julius Wilson, and Faith Mitchell (National Academy Press, 2001).

She is also a guest editor for *Feminist Economics*; a member of the Macarthur Research Network on Family and the Economy; and director of the American Economic Association's Pipeline Project (for the Committee on the

Status of Minority Groups in the Economics Profession). She holds a Ph.D. in economics from Stanford University (1982).

Kevin M. Hollenbeck

Kevin Hollenbeck is senior economist at the W.E. Upjohn Institute, and also serves as the Institute's director of publications. He conducts research in the areas of postsecondary education, workplace education, and school-to-work transition, and is a member of the Technical Review Panel for the National Household Education Survey, 2001. He has recently completed projects on measuring the impact of career preparation programs in South Central Michigan and in Michigan's Kalamazoo and Lenawee counties.

Hollenbeck's recent publications include *In Their Own Words: Student Perspectives on School-to-Work Opportunities*, for the National Institute for Work and Learning, and "Postsecondary Education as Triage: Returns to Academic and Technical Programs" which appeared in *Economics of Education Review*. He received his Ph.D. in economics from the University of Wisconsin-Madison.

Alan B. Krueger

Alan Krueger is Bendheim professor of economics and public affairs at Princeton University. He has published widely on the economics of education, labor demand, income distribution, social insurance, and labor market regulation, as well as environmental economics. He is also the director of the Princeton University Survey Research Center, a research associate of the National Bureau of Economic Research, a fellow of the Econometric Society, and current editor of the *Journal of Economic Perspectives*.

Krueger's work has appeared in the leading economic journals, most frequently in the *Quarterly Journal of Economics, Journal of Labor Economics, American Economic Review*, and the *Industrial and Labor Relations Review*. His most recent books are *Education Matters: A Selection of Essays on Education* (Edward Elgar Publishing Ltd., 2000) and *The Roaring '90s: Can Full Employment Be Sustained?*, which he coedited with Robert Solow (Russell Sage and Century Fund, 2001)

In 1994-95, Krueger served as chief economist at the U.S. Department of Labor. He was named a fellow of the American Academy of Arts and Sciences in 2002. He holds a Ph.D. in economics from Harvard University.

William M. Rodgers III

William Rodgers is the Frances L. and Edwin L. Cummings associate professor of economics at the College of William and Mary, director of the college's newly created Center for the Study of Equality, and a member of the Wilkins Forum at the University of Minnesota's Humphrey Institute.

His research focuses on general issues in labor economics and the economics of social problems. His work examines a variety of topics including the relationship between racial earnings gaps and market-wide earnings inequality; gender inequality; the economics of education; affirmative action; and the evaluation of the impact of labor market policies.

He is the author of numerous articles in scholarly journals and edited volumes on these topics. His most recent book is the forthcoming *Handbook on the Economics of Discrimination* (Edward Elgar Publishing Ltd, forthcoming 2003). He has also offered expert testimony before the Virginia House of Delegates and the U.S. Congress.

Rodgers served as the chief economist of the U.S. Department of Labor from January 2000 to January 2001. He currently serves on Virginia's Governor's Advisory Board of Economists. He is president of the National Economic Association and a member of the American Economic Association's Committee on the Status of Minorities in the Economics Profession. He holds a Ph.D. in economics from Harvard University.

Cecilia Elena Rouse

Cecilia Rouse is a professor of economics and public affairs at Princeton University and director of the Princeton University Education Research Section. Her primary research and teaching interests are in labor economics with a particular focus on the economics of education. Among her many studies, she has examined the economic benefit of community college attendance, evaluated the Milwaukee Parental Choice Program, and studied unions in South Africa. She is currently evaluating voucher programs in Florida and technology-based school programs in Connecticut and Wisconsin.

Rouse's work has been published in the *American Economic Review, Quarterly Journal of Economics, Journal of Labor Economics, Journal of Business and Economic Statistics, Economics of Education Review, Journal of Policy Analysis and Management,* and *Economic Policy Review.*

She is currently on the scientific advisory board of the National Institute for Early Education Research. In 1998-99, she served for one year in the White House at the National Economic Council. She holds a Ph.D. in economics from Harvard University.